THE
MAKING OF AMERICA
SERIES

NORTHVILLE
MICHIGAN

In 1839, the State of Michigan was only two years old. Plymouth Township, of which Northville was still a part, can be seen just due west of Detroit.

THE
MAKING OF AMERICA
SERIES

NORTHVILLE
MICHIGAN

BARBARA G. LOUIE

ARCADIA

Published by Arcadia Publishing,
an imprint of Tempus Publishing, Inc.
2 Cumberland Street
Charleston, SC 29401

Printed in Great Britain.

Library of Congress Catalog Card Number: 2001090225

For all general information contact Arcadia Publishing at:
Telephone 843-853-2070
Fax 843-853-0044
E-Mail sales@arcadiapublishing.com

For customer service and orders:
Toll-Free 1-888-313-2665

Visit us on the Internet at http://www.arcadiapublishing.com

The Village of Northville was incorporated as a city in 1955, comprising 2.2 square miles. The Northville City Hall houses city offices and the local police department. (Popkin.)

CONTENTS

ACKNOWLEDGMENTS

All pictures, unless otherwise noted, are courtesy of the Burton Historical Collection of the Detroit Public Library. Photo credits also include the following: Northville Historical Society (NHS), City of Novi (Novi), and Samuel D. Popkin (Popkin).

The use of the Northville Historical Society Archives, under the direction of archivist Sandy Basse, was greatly appreciated. Thanks also go, as always, to my husband, Ming, and to my parents, Sam and Roz Popkin, for all their support, wisdom, and assistance.

This photograph shows the Globe Furniture Factory in 1927, one of Northville's primary manufacturing businesses in the late nineteenth and early twentieth centuries.

INTRODUCTION

It started two billion years ago, when the earth was still being formed. A mass of rock breaking away from Canada became Michigan's Upper Peninsula; the lower section remained completely under water. Buried as it was, under ice up to 4 miles thick, the land mass now known as Michigan was changing constantly. As the ice began to melt, and thus to move, the landscape became altered by the continuous scraping of soil and rock along the surface below. The resulting deposits from the moving glaciers were called moraines. Moraine Elementary School in Northville is named for the geological site on which it sits.

It was from this ice age that the structure of much of Michigan has been formed. During the time the ice was gradually retreating from Michigan, it left in its wake many of the lakes, rivers, hills, and streams that make up Michigan's landscape. The Great Lakes themselves were created by the retreating ice that covered the earth. At one time during this slowly-evolving process, the melted glacial waters now known as Lake Erie encompassed much of Wayne County, including the westernmost point of Northville.

As the water receded, streams and rivers were left behind. Located in the midst of the Highland Lakes Subdivision is one of these remnants, Silver Spring Lake, the only natural lake in Wayne County. The Rouge River, a tributary of the Detroit River, extends from Dearborn well past Northville and Novi, breaking into several branches known as the Upper, Middle, and Lower Rouge Rivers.

Michigan's draw to newcomers in the early 1800s was due mainly to its promise as an agricultural mecca. The lure of abundant farmland drove many easterners to Michigan's borders to settle the areas leading out of Detroit. Northville was one such location. The first patent taken out on land in Northville was in 1823, and a portion of that land still holds the name of the nephew of the original owner. Gideon P. Benton claimed 240 acres of land around the current Kings Mill Cooperative, including what is today Cass Benton Park.

Early settlers, however, did not arrive until two years later, when a handful of newcomers to the Plymouth-Canton area continued northward. The northern section of Plymouth Township eventually broke off on its own to become the town of Northville.

Northville became a village in 1867. The old Village Hall was formerly the Lapham family home. It stood for over 100 years before being razed to make way for the current City Hall, built in 1963. (NHS.)

Among the town's first settlers were Alanson Aldrich, in 1825, followed by Alvale Smith. Smith sold his property to John Miller, who started the first mill in Plymouth Township. Employees built their homes near the mill, thus laying out the foundation for the town. The names of other early settlers are still evident in street names around town, such as Rufus Thayer Jr., Joseph Yerkes, Daniel and Samuel Cady, William Dunlap, and more.

By 1827, the little town of Northville was truly beginning to take shape. Gideon Benton became the postmaster; Dr. J.F. Davis settled in as the town's first resident medical practitioner. There were two blacksmiths, a tailor, a tavern, and shoe shop. A Presbyterian church was first organized in 1829 at the home of Joseph Yerkes; the early residents intended for it to be led by an itinerant, or traveling, preacher. The first church building, however, was constructed by the Methodists in 1836. Jabish Mead owned the only general store in town for the first few years, but it was soon joined by another store built by David Rowland on the corner of Main and Center Streets.

School was held, like church services, in a variety of homes for a number of years. In 1853, the first schoolhouse, made of cobblestones, was erected, and it was used as a meetinghouse as well. Jacob Ramsdell, owner of a mill in the neighboring Waterford region, served as the teacher.

Within the town itself, other separate communities sprang up. Among them were Waterford—also known as Meads Mill—in 1827 and Phoenix in the 1830s. These districts began with a mill as their base. These small communities did not last long, however, and were eventually absorbed by Northville Township.

Northville remained part of Plymouth Township until 1867, when it was incorporated as a village. But the two villages of Northville and Plymouth were still governed by a single township organization. The large size of the dual township proved unwieldy, and resentment arose between the Plymouth and Northville factions. Finally, in 1897, township officials from both villages met and agreed to detach legally; the separation became official the next year.

By the 1950s, growth in the community led voters to debate the issue of city incorporation. Though it was vetoed by the citizens in 1953, it was approved two years later. Part of Northville became a city in December 1955. As the population expanded, Northville grew in area as well. After becoming a city, Northville was able to annex part of Novi, north of Base Line (Eight Mile) Road, including the area consisting of Amerman School and Northville Estates subdivision.

Today, Northville is celebrating nearly half a century of city-hood. It has grown from a struggling milltown into a picturesque example of modern small-town life.

This book tells not only the story of Northville and its relationship to its surrounding areas, but much more than that. Based on local history articles that have appeared in the *Northville Record* and the *Novi News* from 1989 to 2001, this work also gives personal stories of the town's past: of life in another time, how people lived, what work they did, how various everyday items evolved—and how it all relates to the town of Northville, Michigan. Located in both Wayne and Oakland Counties, Northville, with its neighboring communities, has a vast treasury of tales to tell. Here are but a few of them.

Northville Township celebrated its centennial in 1998. There was a succession of township halls, including a former church building and this structure (pictured here), which later became Meads Mill School. (NHS.)

1. PIONEERS

With horses and wagons, they came. Lugging tools, beds, food, and trunks, they poured into Michigan from the East. They came through Canada, New York, and Ohio, through the Erie Canal and across the Detroit River. Migration to Michigan was common for Easterners in the early part of the nineteenth century and was, in part, one of the reasons that led to Michigan attaining statehood in 1837.

But coming to Detroit and, from there, to northwestern suburbs like Northville, was no easy task. Countless pioneers have recorded their early struggles to the area. One of the earliest accounts was that of cousins William Yerkes and Thomas Pinkerton. They were among the first cautious visitors to the marshy wilderness known then as West Farmington, Michigan Territory.

Making their journey before the opening of the Erie Canal in April 1825, the cousins began their trek in Romulus, Seneca County, New York. They made their way across the state to the port city of Buffalo, where they arranged for passage on the steamboat *Superior*. They landed at Detroit on April 20, 1825, with the most arduous part of the journey still ahead of them. According to *History of Oakland County* by Samuel Durant, the young men "floundered through the seas of mud which lay between [Detroit] and the place of their destination, but they kept resolutely on, and in due time reached the lands on which they afterwards settled."

Arriving in Novi was not enough; they needed to record the deeds back in the Detroit land office as soon as possible, so a return trip was imminent. Historian Durant reported the following:

> Using every effort to reach the city in the least possible time, they took the Indian trail, and hurried on by way of George W. Collins' place, in Farmington, stopped by Thibaud's fifteen-mile house, traversed the muddy swamps, which in many places seemed to be almost bottomless, and arrived in town at night, on the 29th of April, and at the opening of the land office on the following morning made their entries . . .[1]

William Yerkes and his family were among the first settlers of the Novi-Northville area. William's father, Joseph, built this house on his farm along Eight Mile Road. (NHS.)

The men then returned to New York to arrange for transportation of their families to Novi in the next couple of years. When they came back to Michigan, they brought with them William's father, Joseph, his brothers and sisters, his wife, Hester, and their four children. Thus, the Yerkes (pronounced "Yur-keys") family has been around the Novi-Northville area almost as long as the communities have existed, a prolific family still thriving in this area today.

Joseph Yerkes Sr., a veteran of the Revolutionary War, purchased nearly 500 acres on the south side of Eight Mile Road in Northville, close to his son William's farm. William, the original Novi/Northville Yerkes, had ten children. Six of them were born in Michigan, including Robert, born in 1829 in a log cabin on the family homestead in Novi. He married Sara Holmes of Plymouth in 1856. In 1870, Robert sold his farm in Novi and built a home on Base Line Road on a 160-acre tract of land. The Victorian Gothic masterpiece still stands as an elegant private residence. Sara Holmes Yerkes died in 1902, with Robert following in 1914. Both are buried in the Yerkes Cemetery along Eight Mile Road.

Another of William's sons, Charles, was born in 1833 on the family farm. He married Evelina Wells in 1858 and bought a farm in Novi near Base Line Road. His farm was subdivided in 1923.

William Purdy Yerkes, another son of the original settler, became a lawyer, judge, and the first president of the village of Northville in 1867. The next year, he and his wife, Sarah, built the house that still stands in Northville's Mill Race Historical Village. John Yerkes, William Sr.'s brother, married Sarah Thornton, another old name in Novi's history. Their farm was located near Napier and Eight Mile Roads. In later years, one of the Yerkes members took over the Northville Mills and it, along with the millpond, soon took on the Yerkes name. Yerkes Street in Northville is also named for this prominent family. In fact, wherever there is a history of Northville or Novi, the Yerkes family name stands out distinctly. George Yerkes was Novi Township supervisor in 1877. He and his family had a home on High Street; William G. Yerkes, along with another longtime Northville resident, John Knapp, owned a hardware store in town, opened in 1891; W.H. Yerkes was among the first to install a telephone at his Northville residence in 1897; R.C. Yerkes helped organize the Globe Furniture Co. in Northville in the early 1900s; George B., Robert C., and William H. Yerkes were all among the original members of Meadowbrook Country Club when it began in 1916; Mrs. W.G. Yerkes was a trustee of the Northville Library Association in 1926; Joseph, another of the original William's sons, built a house north of Eight Mile Road around 1869. This home, a magnificent testimonial of Victorian elegance, became Novi's only registered historic site for a time. Sadly, after the last family member moved away, the home was left to deteriorate, and in August 1989, the inevitable took place—the neglected building was destroyed by fire, thus causing Novi to lose yet another of its rare nineteenth-century treasures. The Yerkes name, however, continues strong. The remaining homes, the street, and the cemetery are lasting memorials to this important local family.

In 1833, another family that immigrated to the Northville-Novi area left an equally descriptive account of their trip. Colonel Samuel White, also of New York State, came with his wife, Amanda, and their children, Dexter, Thomas, Amanda, and baby Samuel H. Since the baby was too young to remember, Dexter wrote a letter to his brother Samuel over 40 years later describing part of the bold ordeal of so long ago. Rather than taking the

Colonel Samuel White and family settled along Nine Mile Road. Their home and barn, seen here, were built around 1840 and still stand. Both the house and the barn were converted and are used as private homes. (Popkin.)

12

French "voyageurs" were the first white men to settle in what would come to be called Detroit. This is a depiction of Cadillac's landing in 1701.

then-common route of the Erie Canal, the White family went a different way. Dexter recalled the following:

> in the Spring of 1833 . . . we were upon the road in Canada heading for Michigan. A Span of Horses, Wagon, a Colt . . . Three or four Chests, a bundle of Bedding, an Axe or two, a cross-cut saw, a Side of Sole-leather, a Hammer and a few nails and a Shotgun [made up their baggage].
>
> The day we left Lockport I do not recollect or how many days we were on the road . . . The first night spent in Michigan was at Johnsons Tavern ten miles this side of Detroit. The next day, Sunday I think, we arrived at uncle Holmes a little after dinner time. Pretty well tuckered out, Mother in particular. Brother Thomas and myself generally slept in the wagon in the Barn while on the road.[2]

Though settlers like the Yerkes family suffered through "melting snow, the mud and the many obstacles" encountered en route, and despite their "disgusted and rather home sick frame of mind"—according to historian Durant—they stuck it out. Their journeys proved tedious, uncomfortable, painful, and, at times, dangerous, but the travelers remained undaunted and continued to make Michigan their home.

Every early pioneer who came to Northville and Novi in the nineteenth century passed through Detroit. What is today a major metropolitan center was, in those days, a small community on the banks of the Detroit River. Its location on the river, however, was what made it an important port of entry for ships arriving from points east.

French "voyageurs," or explorers, came to Michigan in the early seventeenth century. Among their discoveries were beaver pelts, which were readily available. Favored by Louis XIV of France, the style gained instant popularity and demand soared. Trading posts were established between the French and the Indians. In 1701, Cadillac erected Fort

Detroit im Jahre 1796.

The American flag can be seen flying over Fort Pontchartrain at Detroit for the first time in 1796. Previously, Detroit had existed under the French and British flags.

Pontchartrain in what would be called D'etroit: "Of the strait." The name first appeared on a map two years later. Detroit went from French to British rule in 1760, and after the signing of the Declaration of Independence, the town was made a British center of offense against American settlers. In 1783, Detroit was awarded to the United States by the Treaty of Paris, thus officially ending the war between Great Britain and the new country.

According to the Ordinance of 1787, Michigan was included in the Northwest Territory, which covered the area north of the Ohio River and east of the Mississippi River. Despite this ordinance, Detroit was still ruled under British law and was even considered part of Canada. The British finally evacuated the town in 1796. For the first time in its history, the American flag was raised over Detroit and the first American troops were led victoriously into town by General Anthony Wayne. Detroit's population of 2,200 dropped drastically as the majority of its British residents fled across the river to Canada. By 1799, Detroit was made a port of entry to the United States.

In 1805, the Territory of Michigan was created. That year, however, wrought disaster on the growing town of Detroit. A devastating fire, started in a local barn, destroyed the entire town. Every building in town burned, except one. Though it took the town to a tragic low, rebuilding began almost immediately and Detroit was incorporated as a city the next year.

The War of 1812 was particularly disastrous to Detroit. Near the beginning of the war, for the second time in its history, Detroit was surrendered to the British. It remained under British rule for over a year, until being recaptured by American troops in late 1813. The American flag has flown proudly over Detroit ever since.

In 1831, a 14-year-old apprentice from Ovid, New York, named David Clarkson embarked on an adventure of a lifetime. In company with Captain William Dunlap and five other men and their families, Clarkson made the treacherous journey from Seneca County, New York, to southeastern Michigan. The group began its trip on the canal boat

Shark, leaving on May 1, 1831, for a ride along the Erie Canal. Clarkson's handwritten account of his experiences reveals a good deal about the hardships of pioneer life in the area in those struggling years:

> The company traveled by day-time and lay up night. They were over a week in reaching Buffalo. They then transferred their families and "Puppy Dogs" (of which there were several in the company) to the steamboat "Ohio" bound for Detroit . . .
>
> We were nearly three days in reaching Detroit, and many of the company were seasick. This was the most disagreeable part of the journey.
>
> We landed in Detroit on the 18th day of May . . . The company procured teams to bring them to Plymouth. The women and smaller children riding, while the rest had to walk.
>
> The streets in Detroit was one of continuous mudhole, and the roads through the country were worse if possible.
>
> The trip of twenty-five miles from Detroit to Plymouth took the group two days to accomplish.

Once in the area, organizing a homestead was no easy task, and Clarkson described the process in detail:

> Among the first things needed was an oven to bake bread in, and we tried our hands at constructing one of mud.
>
> We first made a platform of split logs. Then we plastered it over with mud or clay mortar about three inches thick; and placing on this a pile of chips, as near the shape of the oven as we could; we covered it over with mortar, mixed with marsh grass, to make it stick together, and after letting it dry a short time we set fire to the chips and burned them out. Thus baking the clay which made it hard and durable. A roof of bark completed the job.
>
> In a few days we had some bread baked in this oven, and I thought it was the best bread I ever tasted. Over forty years has passed, and I firmly believe I have never yet tasted any as good bread as that baked in the mud ovens.[3]

Clarkson subsequently moved in with the Dunlap family. Though still a teenager, he worked hard for his room and board. Once the family had settled into their "small log house with a stick chimney on the outside," work to clear the farm began in earnest. Clarkson became one of Northville's leading citizens. By the late 1850s, he was acting director of the Northville School Board, serving on the board for many years.

The Great Lakes helped open the door to the West. The five Great Lakes make up one-half of all the fresh water on earth. Lake Superior alone is the world's largest body of fresh water. Though Michigan touches only four of them, almost every pioneer who came to Michigan in the seventeenth, eighteenth, and nineteenth centuries—including those who came to Northville in the early 1800s—traveled on at least one of the Great Lakes to arrive here.

Walk-in-the-Water *was the first successful steamship on the Great Lakes, making her inaugural run in 1818. She helped open the gateway to the west for travelers coming to Michigan from New York and New England.*

Discovery of the Great Lakes by the white man took place in 1615—five years before the Pilgrims landed at Plymouth Rock—when Samuel de Champlain sailed on Lake Huron at Georgian Bay. Fourteen years went by before another lake was explored—Lake Superior, by Etienne Brule—and Lake Michigan was discovered a few years after that. It wasn't until 1669 that Joliet found himself on Lake Erie, and the first recorded voyage on Lake Ontario, by French explorer LaSalle, was made in 1678. The Lakes were so vast that Jean Nicolet, setting out on Lake Michigan in 1634, believed he had traveled to the Pacific Ocean and was heading out on the open sea toward China. These early French "voyageurs" sailed in small open canoes. Even for huge sailing ships, the rough seas of the Great Lakes can be intimidating. It is not hard to imagine how boundless the expanse of the lakes must have looked from the viewpoints of the venturesome "voyageurs."

With the discovery of the Great Lakes came the need for suitable craft on which to sail. Robert Fulton's steamboat the *Clermont*, launched in 1807, opened the gateway to regular travel on waterways, and a new era was begun. Eleven years later, the first steamship sailed on the Great Lakes. *Walk-in-the-Water*, heralded as the first commercially successful steamship on the Lakes, was a milestone in navigation history. After this victorious event, ship owners rushed to get their crafts onto the watery roads to prosperity. After only three years, *Walk-in-the-Water* met her fate, crashing in hurricane winds along the shores of Lake Erie. Her successor came quickly. The *Superior*—the ship that brought William Yerkes and his cousin to Michigan for the first time—sailed the Lakes for over 12 years. During that time, she was joined by a number of other steamers, including the *Henry Clay* in 1825. From a fleet of only 2 steamers in 1825, demand for travel on the Great Lakes was responsible for increasing the fleet to 11 steamboats by 1833.

Lake Erie, the oldest and shallowest of the five lakes, was the scene of thousands of ships heading east and west for decades. Traffic was so heavy on Lake Erie during the 1860s and 1870s that up to 60 schooners per hour traversed the treacherous Pelee Passage.

Though the ships may have been built for the Great Lakes, they needed to be every bit as sturdy as ocean-going vessels. Storms, especially around Lakes Superior and Huron, are still prevalent particularly in November of the year, and can overturn even the most solidly-built craft. Gordon Lightfoot immortalized one of the more recent tragedies in his song, "The *Edmund Fitzgerald*." That ship sank off the coast of Lake Superior in 1975.

The captain of a ship on the Great Lakes, likewise, needs the same sea knowledge and experience as the captain of any ocean vessel. As well-respected as any sea captain, Great Lakes ship captains were prominent citizens in the towns that they called home.

Solomon Gardner was one such personage. A Great Lakes captain in the mid-nineteenth century, he and his wife, though from Detroit, had a home in Northville. Captain Gardner's home on Randolph Street, in what is now part of the city's historic district, still stands. The house, with its spacious front porch and Victorian detailing, was built between 1858 and 1860. Captain Gardner's brother, Benjamin, also lived in town, and his daughter Nettie married Lyman A. Yerkes.

Besides plying the waves of the Great Lakes for commercial use, Captain Gardner also ran a more leisurely venture. In August 1870, a select group of Northville citizens sailed on his steamer *Marine City* to Mackinac Island. The *Northville Record* reported the boat to be "a general favorite with the public, being new and perfectly sound; and withal, officered with men of many years experience in seafaring life."[4] The 1870 trip was a repeat of a similar excursion taken a year earlier. Shortly afterwards, Captain Gardner retired from the Lakes. The lure of the Great Lakes, from the time of Nicolet, has been irresistible to some, and Captain Solomon Gardner, who made his life on the Lakes, was one of those unable to resist their unconquerable attraction.

In 1885, Northville had only one lawyer in town and his name was Elias S. Woodman. The son of Dr. Joseph and Sally Wright Woodman, Elias was born in Rodman, New York, in 1816. He traveled west with his family the same year Michigan became a state, in 1837, and they settled in Novi. His father's sudden death the next year made young Elias the head of the large family. At age 22, Elias Woodman had become the sole supporter of a family of five younger brothers, one sister, and their mother.

Shortly after his father's death, Elias borrowed a dollar from a neighbor to use for legal services to settle his father's estate. The nearest attorney was F.J. Drake of Pontiac. Drake was so impressed by the determined young man, he waived his legal fee and helped him settle his affairs, thus enabling Woodman to repay the dollar to his neighbor on his return. The lawyer had much influence on young Woodman, and the study of law became Woodman's passion. Noted in his obituary as "a man of great force and determination," Woodman was successful in gaining admittance to the Michigan State Bar without ever having attended law school.

Elias Woodman was one of the youngest members to serve on the state Constitutional Convention of 1850, working with the Honorable J.D. Pierce and Isaac E. Crary, advocates and authors of the Homestead Exemption Law and the free public school system. Woodman had married Mary Hungerford of Plymouth in 1840. They raised four sons and one daughter before Mary died in 1868. Two years later, Elias married his sister-in-law, Lavinia.

Woodman's obituary in 1894 praised him as "frank, open-hearted and genial, but firm in his convictions."[5] Part of these convictions prompted Woodman to give the first speech in Michigan urging participation in the War of the Rebellion, later known as the Civil War. A history of Wayne County, published in 1890, detailed Woodman's involvement as follows:

> When the news of the attack on Fort Sumter by the Southern Confederacy in 1861 reached Novi, a meeting of citizens being held at the schoolhouse, Mr. Woodman was called out and made a short speech on the situation, pledging himself to do all in his power to put down the rebellion . . . he kept his promise well, enlisted his own son and went twice to the seat of war and spent his time in camp and hospital, nursing sick and wounded soldiers.[6]

His son's life was—fortunately—spared, and they both returned home to Novi. Elias S. Woodman died in Northville in October 1894 at the age of 78, an honored and well-respected citizen of the community.

When Henry Houk died in Northville on August 29, 1892, he had been one of the oldest residents in the area. Born just one year after Washington retired from the presidency, Houk lived through Napoleon's reign, the invention of the steamboat, the War of 1812, the Alamo, the Civil War, and the Industrial Revolution. Five years after his death, during Northville's celebration of the 100th anniversary of George Washington's inauguration, Houk was honored posthumously as having been one of two Northville men who had been born while Washington was still alive. According to the *Northville Record*, "Of the 56 signers of the Declaration of Independence, 21 were alive at [Houk's] birth. Of the 23 presidents this country has had [at the time of the article], 20 of them died during Houk's . . . lifetime."[7]

A native of Steuben County, New York, Houk participated in his first presidential election when Andrew Jackson ran for president. Houk came to Michigan in 1833 and lived a long, healthy life. Just a few months before his death, he had been visited by his old friend Elias S. Woodman, who reported on his visit in the *Detroit Free Press*: "Henry Houk [was] celebrating the ninety-fourth anniversary of his birthday, splitting wood."[8] He was reportedly feeble, but healthy. Sadly, his health did not last long, but he was successful in gaining the respect and affection of an entire village.

2. NAMES

Northville is unique in that it is located in two counties: Wayne and Oakland. The two counties are divided by Eight Mile, or Base Line, Road. Northville straddles both sides of the line. The first county in Michigan was organized in 1815 and named in honor of General "Mad" Anthony Wayne. Wayne County, in its initial stages, encompassed nearly all of Michigan, as well as parts of Ohio, Indiana, and Wisconsin. It was reduced to its present boundaries in 1826.

Oakland County was organized in 1820. Named for the forests of oak trees that covered the land, the county originally included nearly the entire thumb area of Michigan. In 1818, a company was formed to scout out the forests outside of the tiny fort of Detroit. Known as the Pontiac Company, named for the Indian chief who lived nearby, the brave group was led by Colonel Stephen Mack. Along with a small group of settlers, the Pontiac Company took some two months to travel from Buffalo, New York, to their final destination of Pontiac, Michigan.

According to nineteenth-century historian Samuel Durant, Pontiac became "the first prominent settlement planted in the interior of Michigan, the first one located beyond the cordon of tangled forest . . . which surrounded Detroit."[1] By the end of 1818, the area that would become the village of Pontiac was surveyed and platted. Pontiac became the Oakland County seat early on, and in 1837 was incorporated as a village.

The communities that make up Wayne County had an even earlier start. Even before Detroit was founded in 1701, a large island in the Detroit River, called "Grosse Ile" by French explorers, was discovered and later settled. The first settlement outside of Detroit was just east of the town at a point jutting into Lake St. Clair. Early French settlers named the place "Grosse Pointe" for its geological formation.

The next towns to become inhabited were Southgate and Dearborn, both in 1795. Southgate remained, for the most part, a small farming community up through the 1950s. Dearborn, just west of Detroit, was a convenient rest stop for pioneers venturing away from the city. Dearborn gained its greatest fame, of course, when Henry Ford made it the home of his automobile company in 1915. In 1798, another town was founded and was

General "Mad" Anthony Wayne was an American Revolutionary War officer who led the advance in the Battle of Monmouth, among other notable accomplishments. His name was given to Michigan's first county.

named for Revolutionary War hero John Hamtramck. This town, though surrounded by the City of Detroit, has remained independent of it since its creation. Hamtramck became a city in 1921. Interestingly, the next area that was settled in Wayne County was some distance north of the city. A thriving Indian settlement lived along the banks of the Rouge (Red) River. When white settlers forded the river in 1809, they called the place Bucklin, after the leader of the group. After a couple of name changes, it was eventually, permanently, changed to Redford.

The early 1800s saw a number of downriver communities pop up, including Gibraltar in 1811, Ecorse in 1814, and Trenton two years later. In 1818, both Wyandotte—named for the large Indian tribe that had lived there since the mid-1700s—and Highland Park were established. At an elevation of 847 feet, Highland Park reflects the highest point north of the Detroit River. Like Dearborn, Highland Park gained fame because of Henry Ford, who built his first automobile factory there in 1909.

The years between 1824 and 1827 saw the following towns spring up: Northville, Plymouth, Canton, Wayne, Belleville, and Romulus.

Northville got its name because it is located north of Plymouth, which, in turn, was named in honor of the Massachusetts city where the pilgrims landed. Originally part of Plymouth Township, Northville was joined with the towns of Plymouth and Canton from 1827 through 1834. That year, Canton broke away from the group to form its own township.

By 1867, in opposite corners of Plymouth Township, two tiny town centers had incorporated as villages: Plymouth in the south and, appropriately, Northville in the north. Resentment between the two villages eventually gave rise to a movement to split the township, and by 1898, the two communities were officially divided.

Northville became a city in 1955. Northville's village government had been established long before Northville Township even existed, and voters chose to keep the new city boundaries the same as those of the earlier village. Later annexation of Novi Township property, north of Base Line Road, increased the City of Northville's boundaries, and placed the city into both Wayne and Oakland Counties.

Henry Utley, son of Plymouth pioneers, described the naming of Plymouth in a paper presented to the Michigan Pioneer and Historical Society. In 1832, when the small settlement was growing in population, the first town meeting was held in John Tibbet's barn. According to Utley, this was where and when the name "Plymouth" was decided upon, despite some strong opposition.

Three years earlier, in honor of the first American missionaries being sent to China, a number of Chinese-sounding names became popular in U.S. cities. Utley explained as

Grosse Ile was the first community in the Detroit area of today to be settled by white pioneers. The island in the middle of the Detroit River was discovered even before Detroit's settlement in 1701.

What is now the Detroit suburb of Westland was once a rural farming community in Wayne County called Nankin Township.

follows: "It was at one time proposed to call the town Pekin, as two of the adjoining towns were . . . called Canton and Nankin. But better counsels prevailed, and this Chinese nomenclature was discarded for the more historical and patriotic name which was finally selected."[2]

The name of Pekin was used, though Pekin Township was later changed to Redford. Formerly known as Nankin Township, the area surrounding the Westland Shopping Center became the only city to be named for a shopping center. Taking its name from the successful business enterprise that literally made the town, Westland became a city in 1966. Canton retained its Chinese name, providing an exotic flavor to an otherwise ordinary place.

Many cities in our midst were named for their New York counterparts from where their first settlers came. Some of these cities include Farmington, Livonia, and Salem. Taylor, named for the U.S. president, was settled in the 1830s, as were Livonia and Inkster, which was named for early farmer Robert Inkster. Harper Woods, settled some 20 years later, was named in honor of Walter Harper, a Detroit philanthropist who also founded Harper Hospital. Melvindale received the first name of another local humanitarian, Melvin Wilkinson, after it was settled in 1870.

Homesickness was responsible for the names of nearly a third of the towns in Oakland County. The trek through the dense forests that made up Wayne and Oakland Counties in the early nineteenth century caused many a visitor to dwell fondly on the homes they left behind. Many of the towns they settled in Michigan reflect that longing. One of the earliest communities to be formed in Oakland County was Rochester, named for the city in New York from which the county's first settlers arrived in 1817. More New York clones included Troy and Auburn Hills (originally Auburn Heights), both settled in 1821, and Farmington, settled in 1824. Independence Township was named not for a New York city, but for Independence, New Jersey, in 1833. Birmingham, England, was the inspiration for the Michigan city that was founded in 1819. Incorporated as a village in 1864, Birmingham became a city in 1933.

Other communities took their names from prominent members of society. Ortonville was named for Amos Orton, who built a sawmill there in 1848. He also served as the village's first postmaster. Lathrup Village takes its name from real estate developer Louise Lathrup, who helped found that community in 1926. It became the City of Lathrup Village in 1953.

Clarkston, though located in northern Oakland County, has a connection with Northville. When Nelson Clark and his brother created a town in 1840, they named it for themselves. It soon became a recreational resort because of the numerous lakes in the area. Clark, a prominent fish breeder, later moved to Northville and was instrumental in establishing what became one of the finest fish hatcheries in the United States.

Clawson was named in error. When early settler John Lawson applied for a post office in his name, an extra "C" appeared out of nowhere, and the name stuck. Clawson became a city in 1940. Madison Heights was named for President James Madison, and Benjamin Franklin was honored in the tiny village known today for its cider mill.

Lyon Township was named for Lucius Lyon, a local legislator, in 1832. The southern part of the township was appropriately named, though South Lyon was originally called Thompson's Corners to acknowledge the first settler, a common practice in those days. Noted by historian Durant as a "pleasant rural village," South Lyon joined its neighbors in 1871 when it—like Novi and Wixom—built a railroad depot. This distinction, according to Durant, "gave an impetus to the prosperity of the village."[3] South Lyon became an incorporated village two years later.

Another section of Lyon Township is New Hudson. Never incorporated as a city or a village, it is considered the township seat, with township offices located within its boundaries. New Hudson was first settled in 1832. When the Grand River Road was created two years later, it ran right through the little hamlet. The connection between Detroit and Lansing was a well-used thoroughfare, and various businesses began to flourish along the route. During these busy years, the area boasted a hotel, blacksmith shop, boot shops, gristmill, and more. The road progressed from a rough ribbon of logs for stagecoaches, to a gravel road in the early 1900s, to a paved road in the 1920s suitable for automobile traffic.

Wixom started out as Sibley's Corners. Named for the owner of the farm located in the southeast section of the community, the town later honored another early pioneer, Willard Wixom. He was responsible for platting the town in 1871 for the railroad.

The Meads and the Ramsdells, once contemporaries and founders of towns in the same area, are united again in death, near each other in the Waterford Cemetery in Northville Township. The name of the cemetery is the only remnant of what was once a little town located between Northville and Plymouth. (Popkin.)

The City of Walled Lake has one of the more descriptive names, as it refers to a "wall" of boulders that once bordered the lake. Some believe that Novi stands for the Roman numeral six (No. VI), which refers to the town being the sixth stop on the trail from Detroit to Lansing. Numerous other stories abound as to the origin of the name, but the mystery remains. To this day, no one knows for sure how Novi got its name. Like Novi, Milford suffers from an identity crisis. It is unclear whether the town was named after Milford, Massachusetts, Milford, Connecticut, or simply because a "mill" was established where locals could "ford" the nearby Huron River. The last suggestion, however, is the most often accepted.

Still other Oakland County cities describe their surroundings. Ferndale depicts the many ferns that grew in the area, while Hazel Park evokes the many hazelnut bushes found there. Royal Oak was named for a large ancient oak tree, supposedly dating 100 years before its first settlement in 1819. Southfield takes its name from its location in the county. Waterford was clearly a place where settlers as early as 1819 forded the river. Oxford, on the other hand, was named for the many teams of oxen owned by the early farmers.

Throughout Wayne and Oakland Counties there once existed a number of thriving towns, filled with growth and promise, but destined to ultimately wither up and vanish forever. Springwells Township, now represented only by Springwells Street in Detroit, was one of these towns. Once forming Detroit's southwest boundary between Dearborn and the Detroit River, the township held a place of infamy during the War of 1812, as the site of Detroit's degrading surrender to the British. Greenfield Township, near today's Greenfield Road, created the northern outskirts of Detroit in the early 1800s. Located just east of Redford, this township flourished mainly until the national Panic of 1837, which hit Michigan about two years later. The Kensington Bank was a "wildcat" bank, one that was unable to pay cash on its bank notes. When the bank failed, the city soon followed. In less than ten years the village went from a boom town to a ghost town. A century later, the area known as Kensington once again began to emerge, but this time as a nature center and metropolitan park. All remnants of early city life, however, are long gone.

Northville is the site of yet another of these once-thriving towns. The name Meads Mill is known today mainly as the middle school off of Six Mile near Northville Road. Mead's Mill—also called Waterford—was actually the name of a town once located in that area.

In 1837, two brothers named Ramsdell established the land bounded by Sheldon and Haggerty Roads, Five and Six Mile as a village and called it Waterford. A few years earlier, however, another set of brothers named Mead also settled in the same area and built a large flour mill. They called the place Mead's Mills, making it official with a post office in that name. The two names coexisted peacefully for many years. The town—whatever it chose to be called—had high hopes and a promising future. The Mead brothers' mill produced hundreds of barrels of flour a day, while other related industries were equally successful. In May 1873, the *Northville Record* described the town of Mead's Mill as follows:

> Mead's Mill is a small town on the Holly, Wayne & Monroe Railroad. It is midway between Plymouth and Northville, both small enterprising villages, all within the township of Plymouth.
>
> Mead's Mill is known on railroad stations as Waterford, taking the former for postal conveniences, the latter from its fine water power. It is considered a town of importance in the political world, being the home of the Honorable Winfield Scott, also the native place of T.J. Ramsdell, now of Manistee, who figured largely in the Vanderpool trial, and his brother J.G. Ramsdell, Circuit Judge for Traverse Districts. It boasts of one of the finest water powers on the River Rouge, but running idly away, waiting for some capitalist to invest.
>
> Waterford contains 29 dwellings, a foundry, grocery, post office etc. Wm. A. Ramsdell is the owner of the foundry. Plantation bells are cast at this foundry, which find ready sales in many parts of the state . . .[4]

By the early nineteenth century, Waterford—or Mead's Mills—was a bustling, prosperous community. The mill became a stop on the Underground Railroad, hiding escaping slaves on their trip to Canada from the South. Then, in 1850, the town was hit by disaster. The mill caught fire and burned to the ground. Undaunted, the Meads quickly rebuilt. Their new mill was, reportedly, five stories high and the largest of its kind in the state. Business boomed for several more years in the mill and in the town. Unfortunately, prosperity was not to last. In the early 1870s, another inferno destroyed the mill, and with

Dunlap Street, in the early 1900s, was a tree-lined dirt road, like most streets in town. This street was named after William Dunlap, an early settler.

its fall went the entire town. As businesses and factories expanded in nearby Plymouth and Northville, poor floundering Waterford didn't stand a chance. It, like its ashes, was gone forever. Today, all that remains is a sign along Hines Drive indicating "Meads Mill," the site of the long-ago mill. High up on Franklin Street, east of Northville Road near Six Mile, is the Waterford Cemetery, a small, wooded patch of ground that was dedicated in 1836. Here again the Mead and Ramsdell families are reunited, buried side by side in the town they began so long ago. The towns of Mead's Mills, or Waterford, Springwells, Greenfield, and Kensington have all faded even from memory. Just the names are left behind to remind us that these once-promising communities did exist.

Where do streets get their names? In Northville, some are merely descriptive: High, East, West, and Center. Others take on the names of their locations, like Church or River Streets. Northville's Rouge Street runs along that branch of the river that flows through the city. In the city of Northville, the majority of streets were named after local celebrities. A number of the streets in the historic district were named for early settlers, such as William Dunlap and Daniel Cady, who owned much of the land on the north side of the village. Watson Rogers, a farmer, worked most of the land in the Orchard Heights area, where Levi F. Eaton also had a farm.

Asa Randolph was the head of the Northville Academy and the son of Merritt Randolph, who operated two local hotels in town in the nineteenth century: the Park House and the Exchange Hotel.

Charles Yerkes's daughter Grace Dusenbury became immortal when a street was named for her. Landowners William and Anna Scott were also immortalized in the one-block street that bears their name. McDonald Street was named after another early landowner.

Many city streets honor the names of local officials, such as village presidents Clarence A. Hutton, Edward S. Horton (who was also a U.S. postmaster), Conrad Langfield, and city mayor Malcolm A. Allen.

Attorney William Yerkes, descended from one of the area's earliest settlers, made a name for himself by becoming probate judge in Wayne County and the first president of the village of Northville. Francis Beal headed the Globe Manufacturing Company, one of Northville's early major industries, and was president of the village in 1870–71. Austin Wing was a delegate to Congress in 1827. Mary Alexander, for whom a downtown court is named, was a Northville city clerk in the 1930s. At the end of the 1890s, Dean F. Griswold was a township commissioner and F.D. Butler was a city council member. Other streets were named for local businessmen, such as Carl Ely, William Pitt Johnson, and E. Roscoe Reed, who was publisher of the *Northville Record* at the turn of the nineteenth century. The pastor of the First Presbyterian Church for many years was James Dubuar. George Rayson, an English shoemaker, was active in early village affairs.

As early as 1815, a "base line" was drawn through the state for surveying purposes. At that time, a base line running east and west across Michigan was created in order to

William and Sarah Yerkes' home, built in 1868 on Cady Street, stood there for nearly 100 years before being moved to Northville's Mill Race Historical Village in 1975. (Popkin.)

27

establish a principal meridian for the territory. From this line, nineteenth-century surveyors were able to organize all the townships in Michigan. Years later, a road was created that followed the original surveyors' mark, which still bears the early name and traverses directly through Northville.

Sheldon Road, known as Center Street when it runs through the city of Northville, was named for Timothy Sheldon, an early pioneer of the area.

Traveling west out of Detroit, Timothy and his wife, Rachel, settled in Canton Township in June 1825. That year was significant in the development of Michigan. Two months earlier, the widely anticipated Erie Canal was opened, providing a more direct route from New York to Lake Erie and across to Detroit. Many Easterners came to Michigan via that route, and a number continued even farther west. One such destination was Fort Dearborn, which became the city of Chicago. Enough early travelers passed along the rugged Indian trail in 1825 to warrant the establishment of a Detroit-to-Chicago road. First called the Sauk Trail, the road was known for many years as, simply, the Chicago Road; it is today's Michigan Avenue.

The creation of the road also led to the settlement of many communities en route, and Timothy and Rachel Sheldon were among those who found their Michigan home as a result of traveling this pathway. Like the well-known innkeeper Conrad "Coon" Ten Eyck years before them, who opened an inn along the same road just outside of Detroit in Dearborn, the Sheldons decided to do the same. They built a roomy inn along the side of the Chicago Road which served many a traveler well during the settlement of Michigan in the 1820s and 1830s. The Sheldons probably couldn't have picked a more ideal spot for their inn. As if serving as a convenient resting place for weary travelers passing by wasn't enough, in 1831, approval came for the establishment of a territorial road.

The report of March 3, 1831, described the route of the Territorial Road "commencing at or near the inn of Timothy S. Sheldon, on the Chicago road, in the township of Plymouth, and running thence through the village of Ann Arbor west to the mouth of St. Joseph's river . . ." all the way to the shores of Lake Michigan.[5] The Sheldons remained on their farm, running their inn, at the crossroads of the Chicago, Territorial (now Geddes), and North (later to be called Sheldon) Roads. According to Canton historian Diane Wilson, by 1835 the area became known as Sheldon's Corners. It soon evolved into a small town, including "a one-room school, two churches, blacksmith shops, cobbler shop, two general stores, a creamery, and several well-ordered homes."[6] Timothy Sheldon served his namesake community well, as the first postmaster of the village and a trustee of the Methodist church. When a railroad line was opened in 1837, Sheldon Village was on the route to and from Detroit and Ypsilanti.

The intersection of Sheldon, Geddes, and Michigan Roads, once known as Sheldon's Corners, is today a busy one, more so than Timothy Sheldon ever could have imagined. Writing to his cousin John Pitts Sheldon in 1833, Timothy stated, "the rage for emigration has increased beyond calculation. If one could judge from what the people say in these towns, there would be . . . room [no] long[er]."[7]

Meandering past tree-lined park land from Dearborn all the way into Northville is one of Wayne County's most picturesque parkways. Edward N. Hines Drive was named for Wayne County's first road commissioner, who served in that capacity for the first three decades of the twentieth century. Edward N. Hines began his professional life as a printer, working as president of the long-running Speaker-Hines Printing Company of Detroit. He married Clara Steers of Northville in 1898. Hines made a name for himself as a young man. In 1911, as witness to an accident between a horse-drawn wagon and a still-novel automobile, Hines realized there was no discernible way to determine where the center of the road was. In the accident he saw, each driver had been convinced that they were each on the right side of the road. As road commissioner, Edward Hines was able to make a difference. It may sound simple to today's travelers, but by painting a white line down the center of every bridge, every curved road, and—eventually—every street in his district, Hines established a safety precedent which was adopted all over the world.

Known as the "father of the white line," Hines was made the fifth recipient of the prestigious "George S. Bartlett Award for Outstanding Work in American Highway Development" in 1935. He was honored a year later by the American Automobile Association for his contributions to automobile safety. Hines was to receive many more awards for highway development in the next few years, before his death in 1938. He was responsible for a number of innovations during his lifetime.

Edward N. Hines was Wayne County's first road commissioner. He became known as the "father of the white line," thus helping to prevent head-on collisions on roadways.

The increase of automobiles on the roads demanded better thoroughfares, so the Wayne County Road Commission was created in 1906. Along with Hines on the original commission were automobile maven Henry Ford and Northville farmer Cass Benton. Even before the automobile took over the roads—and his life—Edward Hines was involved in traffic safety. He organized the League of American Wheelmen in the 1890s. This organization of bicyclists, which was a pioneer group geared to highway improvement, eventually resulted in the establishment of the first county highway system in 1893. An avid biker, Hines was also instrumental in the creation of the first bike path in the area. He was able to convince the *Detroit Journal* newspaper to finance a trail running from Grosse Pointe to Detroit along Jefferson Avenue. While courting his fiancee in Northville, it was reportedly common for Hines to bike 100 miles in a day along the bumpy roads to visit her.

One of his first tasks as Wayne County road commissioner was to suggest the use of concrete in the paving of roads, rather than the logs, boulders, and gravel that had covered trails in the past. His idea turned into reality in 1909, when 1 mile of Woodward Avenue became the first paved road in the country. By 1936, half of the streets in Wayne County were constructed of concrete. Hines standardized the minimum width of a traffic lane as 10 feet in Wayne County. In 1912, Hines encouraged county snow removal from the streets, which has become routine practice ever since. In addition, he promoted roadside

John S. Haggerty was a bricklayer-turned-politician, as this 1905 caricature portrays. Haggerty Road forms the eastern boundary line of Northville.

beautification. The name change of Middle Rouge Parkway Drive to Edward N. Hines Drive in 1937 was a fitting tribute to "the father of the white line."

Another road named for a Wayne County road commissioner is Haggerty Road, which forms Northville's eastern border. John S. Haggerty was born in 1866 in Greenfield Township. He grew up in the area, attending school with the young Henry Ford. Haggerty began his political career as the Springwells Township school commissioner at the age of 30. During the late 1890s, Haggerty worked as a partner in his father's brickyard, eventually obtaining the prestigious contract for the building of the Wayne County Courthouse. After his father's death, Haggerty continued with his brickmaking company, branding his bricks with his own initials.

As the new century progressed, Haggerty became increasingly involved with politics. The popularity of the automobile encouraged "the Good Roads Movement." Haggerty was appointed to the Wayne County Road Commission shortly after its formation in 1906. The first project of the commission was the paving of the old Grand River Plank Road. It was paved with macadam from West Chicago to the Redford-Greenfield Township line. The other commissioners favored brick for the paving of their next project, Michigan Avenue. Haggerty's brickmaking experience, however, led him to favor the more durable properties of concrete, which would be able to withstand the road's heavy traffic. Concrete was also cheaper, and Haggerty encouraged its use. He was out-voted on the Michigan Avenue stretch, which was paved with the then-familiar brick paving. He had his way with Woodward Avenue, however. By the end of 1909, Haggerty was made chairman of the road commission and advisor to the State Highway Department. A few years after his initial success with the road commission, Haggerty branched out and went into the banking business. He became a partner in the Springwells State Bank and later co-founded the United States Trust Company, which specialized in stocks, bonds, and business loans.

While Haggerty lived in a stately home in the city of Detroit, he maintained a country residence in rural Canton. The Canton retreat became a gathering spot for many political bigwigs of the era. Haggerty was elected secretary of state in 1926, serving two terms. At the same time, he was also a road commissioner and bank official. The bank he helped found in 1915, the United States Trust Co., was among the first banks in Detroit to go under in the Stock Market Crash of 1929. The Crash and subsequent Depression hit Haggerty's resources hard. His trust company went bankrupt in 1930, affecting several local affiliated banks. His brickyard also suffered, and he was forced to sell his elegant Detroit house. Haggerty moved permanently to his 150-acre farm in Canton in 1933.

After a brief stint serving on the Civil Service Commission in 1939–40, Haggerty retired from politics, becoming a gentleman farmer at his Canton Township home. Though he never married, he was the adopted father of at least ten orphaned children. When John S. Haggerty died in 1950 at the age of 84, his funeral was attended by a number of leading political figures, including former Michigan governor Alexander Groesbeck.

Detroit has Woodward Avenue and Novi has Grand River; in Plymouth, it begins as Plymouth Road, but whatever one calls it, it's the Main Street of town. Back in Detroit's early days—and up to not all that long ago—Woodward Avenue was clearly the major street for business, shopping, and leisure activities in the city of Detroit. In fact, when

Detroit's "main street," Woodward Avenue, was a busy, muddy thoroughfare in 1875.

Woodward Avenue became the first road to be paved in concrete, it served as a model for the rest of the country. In 1830, Novi's business district began around "Novi Corners," the town's major intersection at Grand River and Novi Road. In 1987, in an attempt to bring back that central core to the city, the Town Center Shopping Center was constructed. Then, in the 1990s, another city hub was created known, quaintly enough, as "Main Street."

In Northville, what curves into town as Northville Road takes on the traditional name and style of a small-town Main Street. When Northville's first industry, a gristmill, began along the banks of the Rouge River in the mid-1820s, a small community began to form. Little by little, families moved into the area, setting up homes and businesses in a localized area. With the establishment of more mills, particularly lumber mills, Northville became known as a logging center. Then, in 1832, Captain William Dunlap sold off lots from his farm to plat the village, thus indirectly creating the town's Main Street.

Though the roadway began as a rutted cobblestone street, many of the buildings seen in old photos of Northville's Main Street are still recognizable today. Others, of course, are long gone—from fire, modernization, or expansion. Through the years, Northville's Main Street has been the scene of much change and activity. The late 1800s saw a major building boom in the town. Traditionally, by the early 1900s, the idea of "Main Street,

U.S.A." was receiving some bad press. Main streets in small Midwestern towns were looked on with some derision by the early part of the twentieth century, as witnessed by Sinclair Lewis's satiric novel. By the mid-twentieth century, however, as urban sprawl turned small suburbs into mere extensions of their neighboring cities, the nostalgia for the small town of the past was revived. Walt Disney cashed in on the idea when he created "Main Street, U.S.A." as the entrance to Disneyland, and Hollywood further encouraged the fantasy with popular films romanticizing the scene.

In 1978, Northville's Main Street began a renovation project that changed the look of the street considerably. What had been a typical Midwestern town suddenly, over the course of the next four years, became a showplace of Victorian décor. The four-year project, appropriately named Mainstreet '78, took advantage of an increased tax plan to renovate and beautify the town. According to the *Northville Record*, the state-approved tax increment financing plan allowed the city "to use tax monies resulting from increased property values in the downtown [area] to pay for $1.6 million in improvements."[8] Northville's Main Street remains an example of the ideal Midwestern small town that would be approved of even by Hollywood.

Plymouth's Main Street has undergone many changes since it was seen in this 1905 postcard. No longer in existence are the trolley tracks along the roadway.

3. WOMEN

The pioneers of early Michigan were a courageous and hardy breed. They faced numerous hardships and disasters, but their determination and fortitude helped settle the towns where today's residents now live. Traditionally, it is mainly the men who hold prominent places in the history of their respective communities, but they were not alone in their conquests. Nearly all the early settlers were accompanied by their wives and children, but rarely do those names come to light. Michigan is able to boast of a number of strong women who helped shape its future.

The first of these began with Marie Therese Guyon de Cadillac, the first white woman settler in the land. Arriving in Detroit with her husband and their party in 1701, Madame Cadillac worked in creating the new village at Fort Pontchartrain.

In 1804, Magdalene M. LaFramboise and her husband set up the first trading post in western Michigan. After her husband was killed, Madame LaFramboise continued in the fur trade by herself, making the business one of Michigan's most successful.

Laura Smith Haviland, a Quaker who lived in Lenawee County in the 1830s, helped support the growing anti-slavery movement in Michigan. Her farm in Adrian became Michigan's first station of the Underground Railroad, the route that helped to guide runaway slaves to freedom.

Lucinda Hinsdale Stone, for whom a U.S. postage stamp has been issued, was an educator from Kalamazoo. She began organizing small reading clubs to encourage literacy in women, and she later became the impetus in getting Madelon Stockwell enrolled as the first woman student at the University of Michigan in 1870.

The Northville area was not without its pioneering women, either. Among the most notable of Novi's female pioneers was Sally Thornton. She was a 48-year-old widow when she ventured from New York with her five young children. She was determined to make a new life for herself and her family. The life they lived was a hard one, with her three teenaged sons doing much of the heavy work. She purchased 400 acres of farmland near today's intersection of Nine Mile and Novi Roads. Through Mrs. Thornton's drive and perseverance, the property remained in the family well into the late twentieth century.

Madame Marie Therese Guyon de Cadillac was the first white woman to set foot in Detroit. The Arrival of Madame Cadillac *is depicted in this mural displayed at the Detroit Public Library.*

Other neighboring communities had equally industrious pioneering women. One of the most colorful of these ladies was the first white woman to settle in Farmington. Cynthia M. Collins, born in 1794, traveled with her husband, George, from the East to Michigan in 1824. When their son, J.W., was born shortly after their arrival, he became the first white boy to be born in Farmington Township.

Mrs. Collins was a feisty survivor. An 1881 report of the Michigan Pioneer and Historical Society told of the "great courage and determination" shown by Mrs. Collins in her early days in Michigan.

"Mrs. Collins," the story goes, "once excited the applause and admiration of a large party of Indians by tying up one of their rascally, vicious-looking dogs with her garter and leading it off . . . They applauded the act as a very courageous one . . ."[1]

Cynthia Collins became one of the original members of Northville's First Presbyterian Church, organized in 1826. She lived the rest of her long life in the town she helped carve out of the wilderness, dying at the age of 92 in Farmington.

When the University of Michigan agreed to admit women for the first time into its medical school in 1871, one of the eager young women to march through the hallowed halls was a Walled Lake resident. Sarah Gertrude Banks was born in Walled Lake in 1839. Her parents were among the original settlers of the area, having arrived there six years earlier. At the age of 17, Gertrude graduated from the State Normal School at Ypsilanti as a certified teacher. During the next eight years, she taught at schools in Michigan and

The farmhouse of Sally Thornton and her family was built around 1839 in Novi. This photograph was taken before the house was moved and renovated in 1992. (Popkin.)

Ohio. Dissatisfied with her lot as a schoolteacher, Gertrude grabbed the chance to become one of Michigan's first female physicians. It took her only two years to complete her studies, and she was soon appointed resident physician at the Woman's Hospital and Foundling's Home of Detroit—now known as Hutzel Hospital—as the city's second female physician.

Caroline Kirkland, who became a noted author in her time, came from New York and settled in Livingston County, near Pinckney. She and her husband were instrumental in the formation of that town, bringing literacy and education to a formerly backwoods area.

Banks became active in local and state medical societies, as well as the American Medical Association. After a year at Woman's Hospital, Dr. Banks was given a high recommendation by Detroit Mayor Hugh Moffat to pursue her next endeavor. She worked as a private physician to the wife of a U.S. Army officer. Stationed in New Mexico for one year, she returned to medical practice in Detroit in 1896. Dr. S. Gertrude Banks was best known, however, as a staunch suffragist. Though Detroit women were able to vote as early as in an 1802 local election, when Detroit first came under United States rule, their suffrage did not last long. The right to vote for American women did not come until 1920, but the real fight began in 1848.

At that time, a convention was called in Seneca Falls, New York, led by national suffragists such as Elizabeth Cady Stanton, Lucretia Mott, and others. This session began with a movement that was to last more than seven decades. Two years after the first meeting, the first national woman suffrage convention was held in Worcester, Massachusetts. Mrs. Stanton joined up with Susan B. Anthony at the 1852 convention, and these two women remained instrumental leaders in the fight for women's rights for the next 50 years.

Hoping that national organizations would help out their cause, two groups began shortly after the end of the Civil War. The National Woman Suffrage Association was formed by Susan B. Anthony and Elizabeth Cady Stanton. A similar organization was also founded that year by a Michigan woman. Lucinda Hinsdale Stone was a noted educator, author, and lecturer who, with her husband, taught at the Kalamazoo branch of the University of Michigan. In 1869, she and Julia Ward Howe, who later founded the Girl Scouts of America, created the American Woman Suffrage Association. The two groups merged in 1890, becoming known as the National American Woman Suffrage Association. Various other organizations, national and state-wide, continued to spring up at this time. The Michigan Suffrage Association was formed in 1870, and the Michigan Equal Suffrage Association was organized in 1884.

A personal friend of women's movement leaders Anna Howard Shaw and Susan B. Anthony, Dr. Gertrude Banks spoke unceasingly to various groups about "Equal Suffrage" and was quite prolific in her writings on the subject. Appearing before the Michigan Constitutional Convention in Lansing in 1908, Dr. Banks spoke to the State Association of Farmers Clubs. A transcription of her speech indicates that she brought statistics to the forefront:

> Of the population of the state, fifty-two percent are men, and forty-eight percent are women. During the past ten years the rate of increase has been men fourteen percent; women seventeen percent. Thus you see woman is unquestionably an increasing numerical factor in the life of the state. If, as the farmer believes, she is also an economic factor in producing and ensuring this vast agricultural wealth, why not be just and grant her an equal part in legislature as well as labor?

Caroline Kirkland was one of several women pioneers who made a name for herself in the early days of Michigan's settlements. As a noted author, she helped bring literacy and education to people living in backwoods areas of Livingston County.

Lucinda Hinsdale Stone was a prominent Michigan educator who taught at the Kalamazoo branch of the University of Michigan. In 1869, she was instrumental in co-founding the American Woman Suffrage Association.

The farmers of the state desire suffrage for women first because they recognize and acknowledge its justice. Second. Because they believe women who own farms and pay taxes are certainly entitled to vote and, third, because they believe not only farmer's wives and daughters but every woman who earns her living is seriously handicapped by the lack of the ballot.

Lastly, suffrage for women will increase the farmer vote and thus secure needed legislation for the protection and advancement of these interests which so closely affect the welfare and happiness of the farm and the home, these being the foundation of our national prosperity.

She wrote letters to the editors of numerous newspapers, expressing her belief in "survival of the fittest." She noted that "the progressive woman . . . will become the leader in all social reforms of the day."[2]

Slowly but gradually, states began to grant women the right to vote, including Michigan in 1918. Then, following World War I, a major push in women's rights was made and by 1920 the 19th Amendment was ratified and became part of the United States Constitution, giving women the right to vote at last.

That same year, a nonpartisan organization designed to educate and familiarize women with their new-found political responsibilities was formed in Chicago. The League of Women Voters of the United States was an outgrowth of the National American Woman Suffrage Association, which had been founded by women whose names are still familiar today.

In 1968, a group of Northville and Plymouth-area women got together to form a local league. Two years later, the League of Women Voters of Northville-Plymouth Area was officially formed and soon grew to include the Novi and Canton communities. Through the years, the League had strengthened its position at national, state, and local levels. New issues are constantly being studied and, though the League remains nonpartisan, it does take certain positions on various national and local issues. As of 1974, all citizens of voting age were made eligible to join the League of Women Voters, and—for the first time in its 54-year history—men were welcomed into the League.

When she died in 1926 at the age of 85, Dr. Sarah Gertrude Banks was fortunate in having seen her vision of equal suffrage become reality just seven years earlier. Buried in the Walled Lake Cemetery, Dr. Banks remains one of the area's notable women.

Mary Alexander Court, a downtown street, was named for a feisty lady of Northville. The *Detroit News* did a small story on Mary Alexander in 1959, when she was 68 years old. Born in Germany, Mary came to the United States with her parents in 1891. The family settled in Ypsilanti, where Mary later attended Cleary Business College. She worked as a stenographer for a weighing scale factory from 1907 to 1912. She married a young dentist, Paul Alexander, and they had two daughters.

After her husband's death in 1934, Mary moved to Northville, where one of her daughters was living. Mary Alexander worked as the deputy to the Northville Village clerk, Frederick Hedge, and when he died less than two years later, Mary was appointed to serve out his term. She retained her position by being re-elected ten times without opposition, and continued in the position after Northville gained cityhood. Mary Alexander lived over a century. She died in 1981 and is buried next to her husband, Paul, at Rural Hill Cemetery.

Sarah Gertrude Banks, of Walled Lake, was the second woman to practice medicine in the city of Detroit. She was among the first women to be admitted to the University of Michigan School of Medicine when she began her studies in 1871.

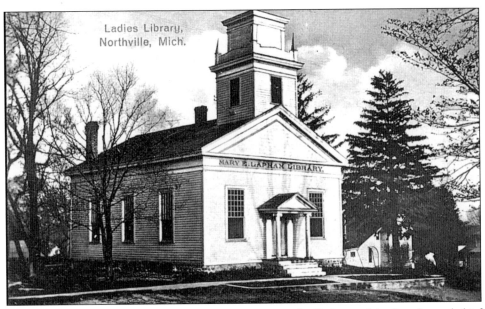

Ladies Library,
Northville, Mich.

MARY E. LAPHAM LIBRARY.

Seen in this 1927 postcard, the Ladies Library in Northville honored its founder and chief supporter, Mary E. Lapham, when her name was added to the former church building.

Over 100 years ago, a group of ladies in Northville established a library, and their library is still flourishing today. Northville's first library began in 1888 as a men's reading room at the YMCA. In May of that year, a group known as the Northville Circulating Library Association was organized, but a year later both the YMCA's reading room and the Circulating Library Association had been dissolved.

The Ladies Library Association was organized in February 1889, celebrating its creation with a benefit performance at the Northville Opera House. This society event was just the first of many such affairs to help out the fledgling library. At that time, one needed to join the library as a member in order to enjoy its books and its services. Library membership, which amounted to about 50¢ per year per person, included 89 ladies of the community at its inception, and books were stored in the former Young Men's Hall. A promotional booklet on Northville published in 1892 proudly claimed that the library "is lighted by electricity, is furnished with a fine piano, antique fire place, easy chairs and everything necessary for the convenience and comfort of its members."

In 1892, the library owned over 1,200 volumes, and membership had grown to 150. Jennie Babbitt served as the librarian. In 1894, the *Northville Record* wrote with pride about the venture:

> The library is certainly alive and booming. . . . A stranger coming into the library Saturday evening would wish no better testimonial to Northville's enterprise and enlightenment than the throng of people so pleasantly and warmly greeting and talking with each other. . . . 150 books were drawn last week and eighteen new members joined.

By this time, the library was housed in the former New School Church on Main Street, a building dating from 1845, which had already served a number of purposes, including the Young Men's Hall.

Mary E. Lapham was probably the person most responsible for the existence and success of that early library. The daughter of Jared and Martha Lapham, Mary had early hopes of becoming a doctor, but was dissuaded by her father. Conceding to his wishes, Mary stayed in Northville, working as a cashier in her father's bank. She did not, however, remain idle. In 1889, she was named chairman of the organization created to form the library committee in Northville. As the donor of the library's original 250 books, Mary Lapham was elected president of the Ladies' Library Association, for which she served nearly ten years. She purchased the Young Men's Hall for the library in 1899. She was the driving force behind Northville's first library, as well as an active member in the Northville Women's Club and treasurer of the Northville School Board.

It wasn't until ten years after her father's death, however, that Mary was able to pursue her dream of becoming a doctor. She studied medicine in Europe and returned to the United States as an expert in the field of tuberculosis. She opened a sanitarium in North Carolina, where she became a pioneer in the treatment of TB patients. She worked tirelessly in the Red Cross centers of Germany during World War I, returning to the United States to work as the research director of tuberculosis at Johns Hopkins University and the University of Pennsylvania.

Though she never again made Northville her home, Dr. Mary Lapham is still considered one of its leading citizens, past and present. In 1904, the Ladies Library Association named their building the Mary E. Lapham Library, in honor of a Michigan woman with courage, strength, and dedication.

The twentieth century brought many changes to the community's library. In 1926, the library was authorized to receive township funds, and thereby became a free public institution. Financial concerns were evident in the 1920s, when the *Northville Record* was requested to investigate the librarian's salary. Mrs. Jennie Cousins, formerly in charge of the abstract division at the County Register of Deeds Office, was employed as the sole librarian three days a week, at a rate of 35¢ an hour, for a total of $300–400 per year. The *Record* stated the following:

> The total income of the library is only $1,200 per year. Out of this amount all
> new books must be purchased, the building must be heated, the subscription for
> all periodicals must be paid, in fact, the entire expense of the library must be met
> out of the $1,200."[3]

By 1934, when the library became part of the Wayne County Library System, some of the costs were allayed by the county. The library was still open just three days a week. Mrs. Bergie Larson was librarian at this time and she—like Mrs. Cousins many years before her—was still earning just 35¢ an hour.

When Northville became a city in 1953, the City and Township began cooperative financial support of the library. The 1960s began a questionable trend in the library's location. In 1964, the library moved from the old church building to the newly

The current Northville District Library, built in 1996, is an outgrowth of the Ladies Library, which began in 1889. (Popkin.)

constructed Northville City Hall. Though this move gave the library more floor space at 3,900 square feet, it was considered only temporary.

Eleven years later, the library was again on the move, to another temporary location at the Northville Square Shopping Mall (now home of the Michigan Gift Salesmen) on Main Street. With almost double the space at 6,500 square feet, it was a nice change but did not last long. Five years later, the library was once again sharing cramped quarters with Northville's City Hall. The 1990s ushered in yet another phase of the library's existence. By 1990, five professional librarians were on staff, the library held 39,000 volumes, and circulation added up to 800 books checked out daily, but the library was small, cramped, and overly crowded. A district library was formed in 1993. During these tumultuous times, plans for a new library began to appear on architects' drawing boards. The vision became reality on October 6, 1996; the grand opening of the new Northville District Library was held amidst much fanfare and celebration.

The new building boasts over 26,000 square feet, 2 floors, a full-time staff of 17 people, and nearly 70,000 volumes plus audio-visual materials. At the time of the new millennium, circulation was booming at 15,600 items checked out per month.

From Madame Cadillac to Dr. Mary Lapham, and others who followed, many brave pioneering women were essential in making an impact on Michigan's and Northville's future.

4. HEALTH

Though nineteenth-century Michigan was often advertised as the land of milk and honey, to some early settlers it was known as the land of chills and fever. Early area settler C.B. Stebbins wrote about his agonizing encounter with Michigan's legendary plague as follows:

> I had heard that people in Michigan had a disease called fever and ague; but I was like the sinner who knows that misery is the usual result of sin, but hopes himself to be an exception to the rule; and I took the risk with little thought. Had I known what was in fact before us, I would about as soon have taken my bride by the hand and walked into the lake as to bring her to suffer what we did.
>
> In July 1839, more than half of the population were on the sick list. My family consisted of my wife, myself and a widow.
>
> Mrs. K. was attacked by ague, and was so prostrated that for a day or two she was deranged. When she was hardly able to walk across the room, my wife and I were, in the same hour, from apparent health, stricken down with what was called chill-fever—a most malignant form of ague. In half an hour we were practically helpless.
>
> Mrs. K. crawled about to wait upon us a little through the day, and during the night we were alone. In three days there were not five persons in the village able to give any aid to others. Some of the time both my wife and I were deranged.[1]

Doctors were of little use, as "our doctor was one of the sick." Recovery was slow, but it did come. "We were able to be up in a few days, but I did no work for three months. Yet, strange as it may seem there was not a single death from the epidemic, in those terrible three months."

In the fall of 1831, just months after young David Clarkson arrived in Northville from New York, he too suffered from the debilitating sickness. He wrote about it in his memoirs as follows:

Every other day about nine o'clock the chills would come on, then I would climb the ladder, pile on all the bed clothes I could find and crawl in, shake for an hour or two and then the fever would last for several hours. The next day I would be around and able to do some chores.

And so it continued for weeks, until I was so weak that I could scarcely get up the ladder to go to bed. The medicine given me was Peruvian bark and brandy, three times a day on the well days, and a good big dose next morning.

Almost every body who came here at that time had the ague and fever. Some would have it very light, others had what they called dumb ague. They had the bones ache and chilly feelings, but did not shake, and the fever was terrible.

Some men would work every other day and have the ague until they wore it out. Sometimes however it wore them out. No pen can tell what the early settlers suffered from this terrible disease. Whole families would sometimes be all shaking or burning with fever at the same time.

Afterwards Quinine came into use, and doctors learned how to treat ague. Then it was not so bad.[2]

In 1873, the *Northville Record* described an ongoing illness that prevailed in the area of Mead's Mill, a town located between Northville and Plymouth. "There is a great deal of sickness through this vicinity which in many cases prove fatal," the *Record* wrote. "Those attacked seem to be taken with a severe pain in the head. Without immediate help it settles on the brain and soon terminates life, but if arrested, typhoid symptoms appear which are long and lingering."

Northville became the site of a number of health centers in the late nineteenth and early twentieth centuries. In fact, at the turn of the century, one of the most popular cures for alcohol, tobacco, and other addictions originated in Northville. The Yarnall Gold Cure, an institution for the "rational treatment and radical cure of the alcohol, opium, cocaine, tobacco and cigarette habits" was begun in Northville in 1892 by Dr. William H. Yarnall. By locating his institute in small, quiet Northville, Dr. Yarnall hoped to enhance his cure with a calming, scenic setting for his patients. Though the Yarnall Gold Cure had branches in other cities throughout Michigan, it was to Northville that people flocked. They came not just for the cure, but because many enjoyed visiting what was touted as "the prettiest village in the state." The setting and Dr. Yarnall's unique individual treatment made for a winning combination. The Gold Cure attracted many prominent citizens, from lawyers and doctors to business people. The overall consensus was favorable for both the cure as well as the location.

A predecessor of Yarnall, which soon became one of its primary rivals, was the Keeley Cure. Also originally located in Northville, the Keeley Institute moved to Ypsilanti in 1892, shortly after the opening of the Yarnall clinic. In fact, Dr. Yarnall began his own center after gaining experience with the Keeley program earlier.

Many graduates of Yarnall's program claimed that they "felt better after being two weeks at the Yarnall . . . than when I had finished at the other institute." The three-week alcohol course cost $50; tobacco and cigarette treatment ran $15 per week; and morphine and opium cases cost $20 per week for the first three weeks—all payable in advance. Room and

The Yarnall Gold Cure Clinic, seen here in 1911, became one of Northville's most successful businesses in the early part of the twentieth century.

board ranged from $5 to $7 per week in a house that still stands on Main Street. Dr. Yarnall's home on Dunlap Street also remains, used today as a private home.

Though today's substance-abuse centers do not generally discriminate between the sexes, the Yarnall Gold Cure was designed to heal "liquor-cursed men" in particular. Some of the "most highly respected and best society ladies" of the community showed their support for this worthwhile cause with enthusiasm. The Yarnall Gold Cure Club was organized at the time of the institute's inception, along with the active Ladies Auxiliary. These clubs provided diversions as well as fund-raisers for the patients in the form of dramatic readings at the opera house and other late-nineteenth-century amusements.

It was a controversial treatment, involving chloride of gold and sodium which, according to its opponents, could cause numbness and insensibility to the patient. Supporters of the program, however, denied the occurrence of such symptoms and Dr. Yarnall insisted his remedy was "as innocent as distilled water." The cure was wildly triumphant, with a reported 96 percent success rate. In just over its first year, over 280 men were treated and released, with only 11 relapses noted. Front-page articles, endorsed by the *Northville Record*'s editor, raved about the treatment. "A Grand Success," a headline exclaimed. "The *Record* is only too glad that it may with much pride point to the wonderful gold cure."

The Yarnall Gold Cure quickly became one of Northville's most important businesses. It lasted for a number of years, until fading out to other more modern advancements in the treatment of such addictions. During its time, however, it reportedly helped a good number of patients. As the *Record* warmly concluded, "It is a public benefit and a work of the highest humanitarianism."[3]

45

Maybury Sanatorium in Northville Township was opened in 1921 to help fight the raging war on tuberculosis. With its school, red-brick houses, and acres of wooded land, it was home to many children, as seen here in the institution's early days.

The beauty of Northville led to the opening of another health care institution. Scenic winding roads lined with elegant tall trees twisted past what might have been taken for a well-planned town. There stood a schoolhouse, beautiful brick homes, a self-contained power plant and water supply, a farm, and even a fully-equipped stage for theatrical performances. But the appearance of wheelchairs, ambulances, and medical personnel indicated the true purpose of the community. Bounded by Seven and Eight Mile and Beck and Napier Roads, the site of today's Maybury State Park was once a leading tuberculosis center, known as the William H. Maybury Sanatorium.

Tuberculosis, an ancient disease, is transmitted from one individual to another by infectious airborne particles, fed by crowded, unsanitary conditions. The City of Detroit was hit by this disease, as were other big cities with tenement areas. As early as 1910, an institution at Eloise was opened as an isolation unit for such victims. As the city grew, so did the disease, and additional wards at Herman Kiefer Hospital and the Detroit Tuberculosis Sanatorium were not sufficient to keep pace with the problem.

Finally, in 1919, a sanatorium in Northville was planned and construction of the massive project began. Run by the City of Detroit Health Department, the institution was known as the Detroit Municipal Tuberculosis Sanatorium when it opened in 1921. It was later called Spring Hills Sanatorium.

William H. Maybury, for whom the institution was named in 1927, was a well-to-do bachelor who had retired from a successful real-estate business at the age of 37. When his cousin William C. Maybury became mayor of Detroit in 1897, William H. returned to public life, throwing himself vigorously into a number of committees for Wayne County. His participation in such affairs finally brought him in contact with the problems of Herman Kiefer Hospital, and it was Maybury who created the tuberculosis unit of that facility.

When the Northville project began, Maybury found himself willingly in the midst of it all, becoming architect, engineer, contractor, and foreman. An in-house publication called his role "a dictatorship . . . [which] for the citizens of Detroit [was] a truly beneficent one."[4] His urging helped develop the Children's Unit at Northville, and the Children's Camp, a summer camp for underprivileged children that lasted until funding ran out during the Depression in the 1930s.

Tuberculosis was a preventable disease even at the early part of the twentieth century, but a great number of people died each year because of the inability to receive such basic needs as fresh air, clean surroundings, and quiet. Northville, far enough from Detroit to be away from hectic city life, yet close enough to be reached in a reasonable time by car, was deemed the ideal location for such a project. Two square miles of trees and rolling hills made up the pastoral site.

By 1933, there were 2,600 tuberculosis patients in Wayne County, more than ever before. But, for the first time—thanks to the new clinic in Northville—the waiting list for those beds had evaporated. As time went by, the need for patient beds in the Detroit area

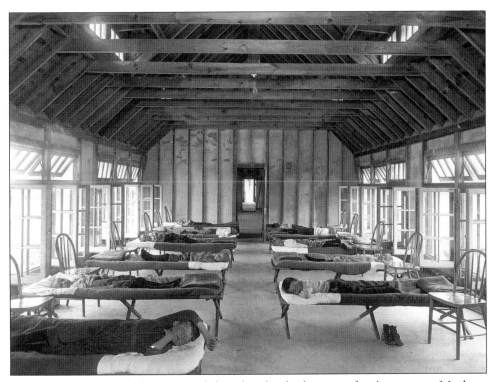

Open windows and fresh air were believed to be the best cure for these young Maybury patients in 1925.

What existed for many years as a center for tuberculosis patients is today Maybury State Park, the only state park in Wayne County. Even before the institution was closed, its natural beauty was evident. (NHS.)

decreased even as the population grew. With continuous advances in the medical field, there became less need for such a huge complex. Discovery of new antibiotics in the late 1940s and early 1950s caused fewer patients to be sent to the Northville center. Death rates also went down dramatically. In 1910, it was estimated that 117 people out of 100,000 died in Detroit alone of tuberculosis; by 1940 it had gone down to 45.5 per 100,000. The disease, though much less frequent than in earlier days, is still with today's population, but in 1983, the national rate was only 8 deaths out of 1,000,000. Of the original 45 buildings erected on the Maybury site, only a few remain. The site has been retained as a state park, but the name of Maybury lives on to honor one of Detroit's noted citizens.

Though Detroit was founded in 1701, it took a long time until adequate health care was formed in the city. Detroit's oldest hospital, St. Mary's, opened in 1850 to care for victims of a devastating cholera epidemic of the year before. In the Middle Ages, trading ships plying the waters of the Black Sea sailed into a Sicilian port with dead and dying men at the oars. This was the beginning of the infamous Black Death, or bubonic plague, which destroyed approximately one-third of the world's population. A similar pestilence swept the planet nearly 500 years later. Asiatic cholera became among the most feared and devastating diseases of the nineteenth century. An 1845 issue of the *Scientific American* reported that, in China, "people are falling [dead] by hundreds daily."[5]

"The Great Cholera Pandemic," which began in India in 1826, spread from Russia into Central Europe, reaching Great Britain by early 1832. Ships arriving in America that year brought the unwelcome visitor. Asian cholera broke out in New York City, claiming over 2,000 deaths. Within a 12-day period in 1832, 6,000 people died in New Orleans, and panic embraced the nation as swiftly as the disease. The plague arrived surreptitiously in Detroit, with seemingly unconnected origins. Like the ill-fated trading ships of the 1300s, the *Henry Clay* was transporting soldiers who had been stricken by a terrible disease. The sick on board were given refuge in the port of Detroit, and the epidemic spread rapidly. Unsanitary conditions in the town, along with low, marshy ground, resulted in a deadly combination. The plague ran rampant through Detroit's military camp; within two weeks, hundreds of soldiers had died. Alarmingly infectious, the plague was quick to pervade Detroit and its surrounding areas. Its effects were soon felt in Dearborn, Plymouth, Livonia, and Farmington.

Fear traveled like wildfire, and many people fled the city, causing greater panic in Detroit's outskirts. Incidents erupted throughout southeastern Michigan. In Rochester, travelers were turned out of a hotel for fear of bringing in the disease. Sentinels stationed outside Pontiac's city limits tried in vain to keep the dreaded infection out of their town. In Ypsilanti, a near-riot occurred when a stagecoach driver refused to let a health officer inspect his passengers. Despite these futile attempts at safety, like the monsters in today's horror films, the disease crept onward, continuing to prey on its unsuspecting victims.

It was reported that a resident of Farmington, a Mr. Barnum, had been visiting Detroit during the reign of the epidemic. He caught the disease and died, and was carried back to his home near Ten Mile to be buried. One of Farmington's leading citizens, Nathan

Detroit's oldest hospital, St. Mary's, opened in 1850 to care for cholera epidemic victims. The hospital's first nursing school graduation class of 1896 is pictured here.

Power, the son of Farmington's first settler, was among those who handled the burial. Unknown to those early residents, the disease was not safe even in death. Power himself became a carrier when, soon after the funeral, his wife and daughter were stricken with cholera, both dying within 24 hours of each other. Sadly, the two were the first persons to be buried in the cemetery donated by Nathan's parents just a month earlier.

In 1834, the plague struck Detroit again, more horrifying than the first time, killing over one-eighth of the population of Detroit. The disease continued to erupt during the next few years. When St. Mary's Hospital opened, it was mainly to care for the cholera victims of this third infestation. Detroit's fourth and last cholera epidemic occurred in 1854, leaving a total of 259 deaths within the brief but fatal visit of only four months. Finally, leaving as stealthily and eerily as it had come, the last of the pestilence was gone, leaving the survivors in stunned relief. Only with the progress made in medicine after the Civil War by Louis Pasteur and others did scientists finally discover how to combat such bacteriological infections that had ravaged the world so unceasingly for so long.

St. Mary's Hospital was originally located on the grounds of St. Anne's Church, at Larned and Randolph Streets, and was first known as St. Vincent's Hospital. When it moved to Clinton Street and St. Antoine, on land donated by Mrs. Antoine Beaubien, the name was changed to St. Mary's. In 1860, the hospital was given a clean bill of health by philanthropist Dorothea Dix in her celebrated tour of the city's health care institutions. The *Detroit Free Press* wrote of her visit, stating that "St. Mary's Hospital was found to possess the characteristics of a well-ordered and beneficial institution. A large number of patients are annually provided for, and no fault could be found with the provisions for their comfort and medical attendance . . ."[6] It existed until 1948, when it was bought by a group of doctors, becoming Detroit Memorial Hospital. Six years later, the former St. Mary's staff and functions were merged with Providence Hospital.

Providence Hospital, which has an outpatient medical center in Novi today, began in 1869 in Detroit. The Daughters of Charity of St. Vincent de Paul established the House of Providence as a home for abandoned children and unwed mothers. It also acted as a maternity hospital. When it was relocated to West Grand Boulevard in 1909, it became a general hospital. It remained as such for nearly 50 years. Then, in 1954, Providence Hospital merged with St. Mary's. In 1965, Providence Hospital moved to its present headquarters in suburban Southfield, on a 22-acre tract near Northland Shopping Center.

Livonia's St. Mary Hospital, which opened in 1959, is not affiliated with the earlier institution of the similar name. When much of western Wayne County was still rural farmland and small towns, one needed to travel to Detroit for any serious medical care. Then, in 1953 when a devastating fire swept through the Livonia General Motors plant, a need for more localized services was recognized. At that time, an appeal was made to the religious order known as the Felician Sisters, who had been sponsoring a facility for the homeless in Livonia since 1937.

The new hospital was to be called St. Mary Hospital. Original funding proved difficult to obtain, but by 1957, hospital officials were able to secure a $700,00 grant that would make the existence of a new hospital in Detroit's western suburbs possible. After gaining further approval from the City of Livonia to install, maintain, and finance water lines along Five Mile Road to the future structure, construction was finally begun in April 1958.

Seen here with its original buildings, Harper Hospital was built in 1863 to help care for sick and wounded soldiers of the Civil War.

At the end of 1959, the hospital opened with 180 beds. Two years later, St. Mary Hospital received full accreditation from the Joint Commission on Accreditation of Hospitals.

For several years, St. Mary's stood alone as Detroit's only hospital. Then, in 1854, the U.S. Marine Hospital was opened. It received "unqualified praise" by Miss Dix in her 1860 visit. The *Detroit Free Press* of September 30, 1860, crowed, "Miss Dix stated that she had visited all the Marine Hospitals in the country, and had found none so cleanly well appointed, and so orderly as the one under the charge of Dr. [Zina] Pitcher . . ." Located at Jefferson near Mt. Elliott, the building served as a hospital through the 1920s. Though the Marine Hospital moved to Grosse Pointe, its original buildings still stand. They remain among Detroit's oldest structures, used today for U.S. Immigration Service offices.

By 1863, the United States was embroiled in the midst of the Civil War, and a military hospital was needed in Detroit to care for Union soldiers. A local citizen, Walter Harper, and his housekeeper, Nancy Martin, donated land they owned jointly to the City in exchange for a place to live for the rest of their lives. In 1863, Harper Hospital was built on land along John R. Street, 1 mile north of downtown Detroit. It opened a year later as a general hospital to care for sick and wounded Michigan soldiers. The original post–Civil War structure was replaced in 1884 by a distinctive red-brick building. This wing of Harper Hospital, which contained what would become the oldest existing operating theater in the country, was used for hospital offices until 1977, when it was torn down to make room for its new additions.

A few years after Harper Hospital was built, yet another hospital opened in the city. Known today as Hutzel Hospital, Woman's Hospital and Foundling Home was founded by and for women in 1868. Like Harper, today it makes up part of the Detroit Medical Center.

Grace Hospital was built in 1888, right next door to Harper. Founded by Detroit law partners James McMillan and John S. Newberry, the hospital was named for the daughter

Located along John R. Street in Detroit, the original Harper Hospital building has long since been replaced by modern facilities at the same location.

of one of the founders. It was designated a homeopathic hospital. In the early days of their existence, the two neighboring hospitals, Harper and Grace, used to vie for the services of patients, with ambulance-racing contests to see who could get to the patient first. The two hospitals have since learned how to coexist more compatibly, and are now part of the Detroit Medical Center.

When hospital reformer Dorothea Dix proclaimed Detroit's poorhouse to be the most deplorable of its kind, her remarks shamed civic leaders into action. In recording her reactions to the conditions of the Wayne County Poorhouse, the *Detroit Free Press* wrote the following: "There were about 200 paupers in the institution in various stages of filth and laziness . . ."[7]

The first patients to be labeled "insane" were admitted to the Wayne County Poorhouse in 1841. The state's first "insane asylum," however, was built on 178 acres of land in Kalamazoo. Known today as Kalamazoo Psychiatric Hospital, it admitted its first patients in 1859. The Wayne County Asylum at Eloise opened in 1868. The Eastern Michigan Asylum, located in Pontiac, first admitted patients in 1877. It was followed four years later by the Traverse City State Hospital. Other mental health centers opened in the late nineteenth and early twentieth centuries, including the state orphanage in Coldwater in 1874; two facilities in 1895, which included an Upper Peninsula center in Newberry; a mid-state center in Caro in 1913; and the Detroit Psychiatric Institute, which opened in 1915.

For the next 30 years, these few facilities were all that served the state's mental patients. Then in 1931, the largest organization was opened. Situated on over 1,000 acres of land, the Ypsilanti State Hospital provided beds and service for many needy souls. According to *MSEA News*, a state publication of 1956, the national average for beds for the mentally ill per 100,000 was 340; Michigan's ratio was only 140 per 100,000.

Thus, in the mid-1940s, a site was selected in Northville Township covering over 500 acres near Seven Mile and Haggerty Roads. Work progressed slowly, and in 1950 Dr. Philip Brown became the hospital superintendent. When the doors opened in 1951, a massive public relations program was instituted "to help bridge the general lack of understanding between the public and the hospital." The campaign was successful in that it brought a number of area volunteer groups to donate their time to the hospital. Known as Northville State Hospital, the name was changed to Northville Psychiatric Hospital in 1995. In 1956, another mental health facility came to Northville Township. Hawthorn Center, established as a psychiatric treatment facility for emotionally disturbed children, opened adjacent to the state hospital buildings on Haggerty Road. Today, Northville Psychiatric Hospital and Hawthorn Center are but two of over 20 organizations operated by the Michigan Department of Community Health. Mental health services are available in every county. Even Dorothea Dix would approve.

Hospitals are important for healing the sick, but many people feel the need to heal themselves. Far below the surface of the ground, a natural bubbling spring became one of Northville's most popular attractions. Located near the old Ford Plant on East Main Street, the spring was believed by many to contain miraculous healing qualities. Even today, people come daily to fill up jugs and bottles with water—whether it is medicinally beneficial or not. The spring, sometimes known as the Silver Spring Fountain, has been providing free water for Northville-area citizens since the turn of the century.

The water was once bottled and sold commercially. "Silver Springs Mineral Water" was served in area restaurants and hotels. In the early part of the twentieth century, the *Northville Record* reported that "The springs east of the [Pere Marquette Railroad] depot also supply hundreds of gallons of purest water daily to the city of Detroit. The large bottling plant adjacent to the springs is an interesting point for visitors. The business is owned and operated by the Silver Springs Water Company."[8]

According to the *Detroit News*, "During World War I, major Detroit hotels and area restaurants filled five-gallon jugs regularly to serve their customers." Former Northville mayor Mike Allen was quoted as remembering the following: "The Pere Marquette

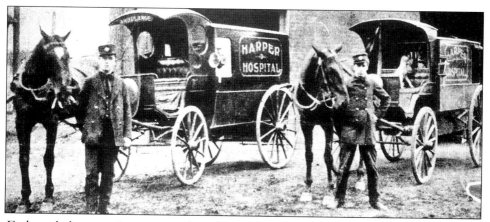

Early ambulance service was carried out by horse-drawn vehicles along unpaved roads.

Railroad used to carry a sign in their dining car which read, 'We serve only Northville spring water'. . . The Nesbitt [Soft Drink] Co. used the same water to make its orange soft drinks."[9]

The spring has been a popular drinking spot for decades. In 1948, the Northville Rotary Club cleaned up the area around the spring, creating Rotary Park. In 1963, construction at nearby Highland Lakes subdivision caused the well to run dry for the first time. Five years later, the Northville Rotary Club once again came to the rescue by financing a new well to be drilled at the site. The *Northville Record* explained as follows: "A good supply of water was found 467 feet deep, but it was no longer free flowing and an underground pump was installed at that time."

In the early 1900s, the spring simply bubbled up out of the ground. Later, a pipe was installed and a drinking fountain was created. By the 1960s, a cobblestone fountain was built around the well, and later a wooden roof was constructed for further protection. With the new well intact, the fountain once more became a popular site in the town, spewing forth water for the next 20 years. Then, in 1988, came a drought that hit most of the country, and Northville's "old faithful" dried up once again. Months went by until the devastating nationwide drought was finally over and the waters of Silver Spring Fountain again ran free.

A promotional booklet from 1892 advertised Northville as a place "where there are living streams of sweet pure water, laden with health-giving minerals." The hills of Northville, the booklet goes on to say, "abound in every direction with magnificent subterranean springs embodying in their constituent parts almost every conceivable mineral ingredient which is known to be efficacious in medical jurisprudence."[10] It may have been merely a flowery public relations ploy, but for many Northville water-seekers, it wasn't far from the truth.

The Detroit News *recorded the following regarding Northville's well on August 1, 1948: "Town wells are common in Italy and Syria but here is one much closer to home. Located on the main road between Plymouth and Northville, residents of both town[s] come here with bottles of milk cans for drinking water supply."*

5. Education and Church Life

In 1853, the first schoolhouse was built in Northville. The first teacher was Jacob Ramsdell, who, according to reminiscences by Northville pioneer David Clarkson, believed in corporal punishment, "and was not slow in demonstrating his belief."[1] Such authoritarian behavior was not uncommon in early American schools. In Detroit's early days, corporal punishment was a matter of course. B.O. Williams, son of leading Detroit citizen John R. Williams, attended grade schools in Detroit between 1816 and 1819. His school experiences could have come out of a horror movie. The first school he attended, in the spring of 1816, was kept by Mr. and Mrs. Goff, located in downtown Detroit on the corner of Bates and Larned Streets. "Mr. Goff," wrote Williams, "[was] a short, thick set, red-faced man [who] presided over the boys' room with rules and rope . . . The rope and ferrule was generally applied until the boy begged for mercy." Goff's drunken cruelty eventually brought on a conspiracy when a group of the largest students took their revenge upon their inebriated instructor "like an enraged swarm of bees, with fisticuffs, kicks, pinching, biting." Thus ended the Goffs' school, which was Detroit's first English school for young children after the War of 1812.

By the fall of 1816, young Williams was enrolled in another school run by Mr. Danforth, who boarded with his family. "Mr. Danforth was a small, waspish, violent-tempered man, and I was nearly pounded to death by him," Williams wrote. "He would box my ears, frequently knocking me off the bench into the fireplace, merely for lounging, or leaning over to rest, as sitting on the high bench was a great torture to me, I being then not quite six years old." Besides the brutal boxing of Williams's ears, Danforth frequently threw rulers at students and "one day threw an open penknife at a scholar." Danforth was summarily dismissed from his duties and was last seen crossing the Detroit River into Canada.[2]

By the 1850s, discipline in Detroit schools hadn't changed much, with students still having the palms of their hands "warmed with a ruler." Others who misbehaved would find themselves seated upon a chair in the corner, wearing a pointed dunce cap, to be ridiculed by their peers. Despite the lack of legislation restricting the use of

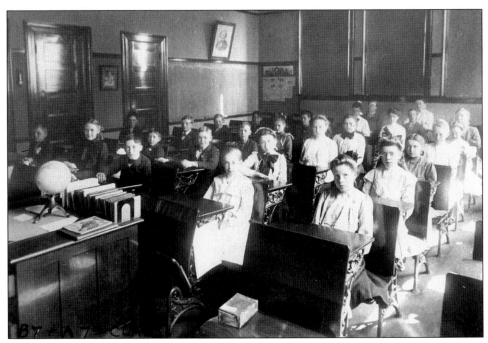

This early-twentieth-century photograph of a Detroit classroom shows a roomful of neatly-attired, attentive schoolchildren.

corporal punishment in the schools, some nineteenth-century teachers were worthy of their profession.

Novi's first school was run by Hiram Wilmarth in the winter of 1827–1828. According to Robert Yerkes, in his history of Novi, "Mr. Wilmarth was an excellent teacher." But even Novi schools had their share of terrors. Yerkes mentions another schoolhouse built a few years later. This school had a trap door in the center of its log floor. "Under this trap door . . . was an excavation, the dirt being thrown back against the logs on either side. By whose order this infernal pit was made, I do not know," Yerkes wrote, "but I do know it was the cause of anxiety to me in my very early days . . . this pit was used as a place of punishment for the scholars."[3]

From educational ideas that proposed complete freedom and total lack of discipline for children to martinetism that caused mutiny among the students, education has come a long way. The Northville and Novi school districts today are among the best in the state, with up-to-the-minute classrooms and equipment for every subject. But both of these communities had modest beginnings as far as schoolhouses are concerned. Children from Northville, Novi, and other area communities attended one-room schools, with all grades taught by one teacher only.

Located near the corner of Taft and Nine Mile Roads were the remains of what was once Novi's Chapman School. Part of Novi School District No. 7 in the 1800s, the school served as many as 47 students in 1870, and as few as 12 by 1885. A few years later in 1899, a "social" was held to benefit the school.

In 1955, Novi Township residents voted to annex Chapman School to the Northville Public School System. According to Northville's former Moraine School principal Donald VanIngen, Chapman School was never used as a school by the Northville School System. It was a one-room schoolhouse used for storage only. VanIngen remembered it being used as late as 1963, in fact, to store desks and other items. By 1997, the remains of many of these items, rusted and falling apart, were still able to be seen on the site, along with crumbling concrete steps leading to nowhere.

Originally located on Currie Road in Salem Township, the one-room Wash-Oak School served children of rural Washtenaw and Oakland Counties. It was built in 1873 and was used as a school for nearly 100 years. The last small class of students attended school there in 1966. After it was vacated and later vandalized, Wash-Oak School was given a new life. In 1975, it was moved to the newly-organized Mill Race Historical Village in Northville. There it was renovated and restored and stands as a symbol of a past life.

A one-room schoolhouse was once located on Seven Mile Road and Meadowbrook in Northville Township. Known as Hinman School, it existed well into the twentieth century. For a few years during World War II, Rosella Lee taught school there, in an experience that she found to be unusual as well as enjoyable, according to an oral history tape available at the Northville Public Library. Part of the Wayne County School System, Hinman School was in Northville's District No. 6.

Washtenaw and Oakland County youngsters attended the Wash-Oak School from 1873 to 1969. It has been restored and is part of Northville's historic village. (Popkin.)

Stone School, named for a person and not for the material, was made of wood, as were most of the one-room schoolhouses. This school was located at Ten Mile and Napier Roads, and after its time as an education center served as a church for many years.

Other area schools, including Walker School at Six Mile and Angle Roads; Geer School at M-14 and Gottfredson in Plymouth; and one at Meadowbrook and Thirteen Mile Roads in Novi were all converted into private homes in later years. As the population grew, so did the schools. The one-room schoolhouse is a thing of the past, but many of them were used by students for a century or more.

While schools in Novi have been given colorful descriptive names, such as Village Oaks, Novi Meadows, Novi Woods, Parkview, and Orchard Hills, the schools in Northville have taken names from a variety of sources. Amerman School was named for former Northville school superintendent Russell H. Amerman. Russell Amerman served as president of the Northville Rotary Club in 1937, and his life was chronicled in *A Centennial History of Michigan*, published that same year. He was superintendent of Northville schools from 1933 until 1964. The school that bears his name was built in 1955.

Cooke Middle School opened later that same year. Ida B. Cooke, the school's namesake, grew up in Northville and attended Northville High School in the early part of the twentieth century. She became a teacher and librarian in the Northville school system and lived to attend the dedication ceremonies of the school named in her honor.

Meads Mill Middle School takes its name from a former town that was located in that area. The Mead brothers, as mentioned in chapter one, settled around what is now Six Mile and Northville Roads in the 1830s.

Moraine School describes the geological site on which it sits. First opened in 1967, the school was built to service 350 students in grades one through five. Winchester School in

Stone School, located at Ten Mile and Napier Roads, served as a church for many years after its purpose as a school ended. (NHS.)

Meads Mill School was once located in the former Northville Township Hall. (NHS.)

Northville Township was named for the subdivision near which it is located. Northville's Board of Education offices are located in what was once known as Main Street School. Though the building was erected in 1937, it stands on a site that has seen a school since Civil War days.

Silver Springs, now the name of an elementary school, was once the name of a prosperous water bottling company in Northville. Located east of the railroad tracks, Silver Springs Water Company was established in 1928. The business itself ceased years ago, but its name goes on in the school located on its property.

Northville's Union School, the town's first high school, was built on this spot in 1865, serving students from both Northville and Novi for many years. The first high school graduation took place in 1868, when one student, Alice Beal, received her diploma. Amanda Curtiss was the only graduate in 1870, and it was three more years before the school had more than one graduate: three students matriculated from Northville High School in 1873.

In 1893, "just half a dozen" students graduated from Northville High School. They included Mabel Clark, Marguerete Thompson, Thad Knapp, Ralph Horton, Hoyt Woodman, and Roy Smith. Some of their names are still familiar today, remembered as local streets.

The current school colors of black and orange go back a long way in Northville High's history, but they had not been chosen quite yet. The *Northville Record* reported that the 1893 class colors were pink and blue; the class flower was the sweet pea. The presence of three young men graduating from the high school was regarded as "rather a novel sight." According to the *Record*, it had been three years since a "gentleman" had graduated from the Northville schools.[4]

HIGH SCHOOL   NORTHVILLE MICH.

This view of Northville Union School was taken in 1904, three years before it was turned into an elementary school. This building was destroyed by fire in 1916.

When a new high school was built in 1907, the Union School was transformed into an elementary school. What is now known as Old Village School was built in 1916 to replace the Union School that was destroyed by fire earlier that year. Built at a cost of $75,000, it was remarkable in that it housed Northville's first school gymnasium. This new building became Northville's high school, while the older structure was converted into the elementary school.

Twenty years later, fire struck once again and the elementary school—the old building regarded by many at the time as a "fire hazard"—burned to the ground. It was at this time that Main Street School was built, dedicated in April 1937. An addition increased the school's space in 1949. After a new high school was completed on Center Street and Base Line Road in 1959, a remodeled Main Street School became the town's new junior high, later housing Board of Education offices as it does today. By 1969, Northville High School had a graduating class of nearly 900 students.

The growing population in Northville near the turn of the twentieth century brought on changes once again to Northville's school system. A new high school was recently built in the township, on Six Mile Road, to accommodate the expanding number of students moving into the area. The last class to graduate from the 1959 structure matriculated in 2000; the school was immediately converted to Hillside Middle School.

Up to the late 1990s, at the corner of Five Mile and Sheldon Roads in Northville Township, were the remains of several large red-brick buildings. Located amidst overgrown trees and shrubs on over 1,000 acres of land, those crumbling, decrepit shells of structures once made up the Wayne County Training School for mentally and emotionally ill youngsters. The buildings dated back to 1924–1926.

A Michigan State Training School located in Lapeer served the entire state for special education to such handicapped children up to 1919. Only a little over 100 children were able to be cared for at Lapeer, and in 1919, over 500 children statewide had been recommended for commitment. In 1921, an act was passed that gave permission to any county in the state to provide for the care, custody, and maintenance of "feeble-minded persons" within that county. Three separate bonds passed, at $1,000,000 each, enabling the construction of the facilities in Northville to handle Wayne County.

The Wayne County Training School for Feeble-Minded Children had a callous name, but well-meaning intentions. When it was first proposed in 1923, the insensitivity of newspaper editors was clear when they exclaimed, "Experts Visit Morons Home." The *Detroit Free Press* stated, "The nation's greatest authorities on feeble-mindedness gave their attention Saturday afternoon to the plans for the Wayne County Training School, the local school for morons to be built on a tract of 1,004 acres, the site of 24 farms, on the main road between Northville and Plymouth . . ."[5]

By 1926, nearly all the construction had been completed, and a number of youngsters originally committed to Lapeer were sent to the new facility in Wayne County. William Maybury, superintendent of the Tuberculosis Sanitorium, which opened in Northville

The new Northville High School, opened in the fall of 2000, was built to handle the population explosion in the city and the township. It is located on Six Mile between Sheldon and Beck Roads. (Popkin.)

The Wayne County Training School, situated on a heavily wooded tract of land in southern Northville Township, was designed to help troubled urban youngsters. After it closed, it was left to decay for many years before being demolished to make way for a new housing subdivision. (NHS.)

four years earlier, supervised the construction of the training school. The complex was extensive, as described by the *Free Press*:

> Most of the buildings are two stories in height. In front of all is the Administration Building, and on its right the hospital and assembly building or clubhouse. Behind it are the grammar school, industrial school for boys and industrial school for girls. Further back there is the service building, containing the kitchen, the laundry, warehouse, garage and power plant, with a smokestack of brick that looks like a monument . . . Finally there are 16 dormitories, eight for boys . . . and eight for girls . . . at the border of a wood, each with a capacity of 50.
>
> Beautiful views may be had from any of the buildings, for the site is 884 feet above sea level, and, with the exception of the Tuberculosis Sanitorium, the highest land in Wayne County . . ."[6]

Dr. Robert H. Haskell, former superintendent of the Ionia State Hospital, was appointed medical superintendent of the Northville facility. By the 1930s the institution was equipped to care for about 800 children. The Depression-wrought 1930s brought criticism of the tax dollars that were being spent at the school. "Officials live like monarchs at Northville," announced the *Detroit Free Press* in July 1932. The superintendent, assistant supervisor, and educational director's residences reportedly cost taxpayers nearly $50,000 each, along with luxury automobiles and even a chauffeur.

The majority of children came from homes in Detroit, but most children from outside the city tended to live in Wyandotte or Hamtramck. The average age of the children was about 12 years old, though boys and girls as young as 6 and up to age 16 were also admitted. The goal of the training school was to enable previously dysfunctional young people to become fully operational members of society. According to the school's annual reports, it was successful for most of its residents.

Though originally designed for "mentally deficient" youngsters, there were a number of delinquent boys and girls as well, many coming from single-parent homes where the parent was unable to cope. The *Detroit Free Press* lauded the results of the school in a headline in the 1930s that read, "Human wrecks salvaged by Wayne County School." The *Detroit News* proudly reported that the "insight into the workings of the school and vocational pursuits followed by the handicapped children" were evident in their "amazing handicraft," displayed in a special show at the downtown J.L. Hudson store in 1932. Christmas pageants and the annual Children's Day were also exhibits of the talents of the youngsters, with songs, stories, poems, and plays performed by and for the children.[7]

Among the training provided at the school were typical classroom lessons combined with a working farm. It was believed that these urban children would gain strength of body and character by working the fields. They were taught every type of farming activity, from hand work to machine work, laboring "long, hurried and hot hours," seeing the harvest from planting to reaping. Other children were employed in the dairy, and all of them took turns in "incidental jobs" such as weed cutting, fence repair, hog care and feeding, and even butchering. What sounds uncomfortably like child labor was considered healing to these ailing youngsters, and the Wayne County Training School was praised for its efforts.

With changing times came changing needs. The *Northville Record* of October 18, 1956, wrote of tentative plans for a "2,500 bed hospital for mentally-deficient children to be built south of Northville during the next few years . . . The hospital, to be known as the 'Plymouth State Home and Training School,' will be constructed on Phoenix Road (Five Mile), extending west from Hines drive . . . The site will cover 250 acres of Wayne County Training School property which would be turned over to the state for a token price."

The Michigan legislature authorized the development of the Plymouth State Home and Training School in 1956. In 1972, the name was changed to Plymouth Center for Human Development. It was under the jurisdiction of the State Department of Mental Health. The hospital provided care and treatment for mentally handicapped children and adults.

In 1957, the Wayne County Training School made national headlines when it became the first institutional day school for mentally challenged youngsters in the country. Newspaper articles boasted of the overall success of the training school and a staff member described the benefits of the program as follows:

> All our 700 children have shown signs of incorrigibility before coming to us . . .
> We give the children work which they can do because this restores the
> confidence, the pride and the signs of accomplishment which they have lost
> because of their deficiencies.

The paper continued, "Boys and girls who once seemed doomed to become social misfits, if not positive menaces, are being reclaimed for society at the Wayne County Training

School at Northville."[8] The Wayne County Training School closed in 1974. The last of the old red bricks are now gone, but the story of the buildings is not forgotten.

Religion came to Northville, as it did to other area communities, in the form of early circuit riders. Religious meetings were held wherever available—in private homes, schoolhouses, or even barns. In 1829, the Reverend Erie Prince made his way to Northville as a Presbyterian minister. Services were held in the home of Joseph Yerkes, alternating between his house and the barn. Sponsored by the American Home Missionary Society (AHMS), Prince traveled from Plymouth to Novi and Farmington in a regular circuit. Times were not easy for these traveling ministers. In exchange for his spiritual aid, Prince was offered the sum of $125 by the farmers of the area. After a year, however, he had been paid only $15. This lack of funds became a constant bane for him. To defer expenses, Prince had to rely solely on the AHMS for financial support for himself and his family. He wrote the following to the AHMS:

> I am satisfied that this is all the people are able to pay. At the meeting there was an understanding that I could not continue with them unless assisted by the Missionary Society. From these circumstances I request your Committee if they think proper to grant me a commission of $100 to labour twelve months in this place, as Gospel minister. This will only support my little family with the rigid economy.[9]

In his own words, Prince accomplished a great deal in the area, and by 1830, he was finally granted a commission from the Society, though it was not as substantial an amount as originally desired. Despite his financial misgivings, Erie Prince remained in the Northville-Novi-Farmington area. After five years of service, he began to spend more time in Novi. Prince eventually made Farmington his home, joining in community affairs and even serving as township supervisor for three years.

Reverend Erie Prince was succeeded in 1830 by the Reverend Ansel Bridgman. Settling in Farmington on the advice of the AHMS, Bridgman's territory included Farmington, Northville, and Plymouth. According to Bridgman, Prince had "abandoned" the people he was supposed to be serving, people who were expressing a desire to have a missionary sent to them.

Writing to the AHMS in November 1830, Bridgman, like Prince before him, felt the strain of bringing religion to the pioneers. Of the 1,500 inhabitants of his circuit area, Bridgman lamented that "few among them . . . call upon the name of the Lord, or pay any regard to religion. The trials of a faithful missionary are great," he went on, "sometimes they appear almost overwhelming." He complained that "A dark cloud hangs over this part of Zion" but had faith that he would be the one to provide enlightenment to the lost souls of Michigan's wilderness.[10]

Methodist services were also held in various locations in the early nineteenth century. Northville pioneer David Clarkson wrote, "The first quarterly [Methodist] meeting I attended was held in Rufus Thayer's barn. Elder [James] Gilruth preached. Anyone who could get in sight of the barn would have no difficulty in hearing the sermon." Though Clarkson called the Methodists in those days "sincere, honest, zealous, hearty and noisy

M E CHURCH NORTHVILLE MICH.

Northville's Methodist church was built in 1885 and is seen here in its early years.

in their profession," other local residents did not find their presence in the community quite as welcome.[11] When they began in the 1830s, Methodist church services were held in temporary locations before a permanent structure was built in 1836. The small frame building sufficed until a new church was erected in 1885 on Center Street. It was later sold and has been used in recent years as a commercial enterprise.

What began with missionaries, circuit riders, and religious meetings held in Northville-area barns, gradually grew to include several permanent places of worship in the town. Northville's earliest church, the First Presbyterian, was organized in 1829, just four years after the town's first settlers arrived. In 1831, on land donated by early pioneer Daniel Cady, construction of a small wooden church building began. In 1838, the church became involved in a theological split within the Detroit Presbytery. Two rival factions were created: the Old School was the conservative side; the New School was the liberal branch. When land was donated by a conservative member to build a church, the fate of that branch was settled.

However, there were enough New School members in the area to organize a second Presbyterian church in Northville. The church this second group constructed in 1845 was called the New School Presbyterian Church. After only four years, the New School members decided to return to the original church. Meanwhile, the Old School members had updated their own small church building with a new brick structure in 1845. The present structure on Main and Church Streets dates from the 1870s.

The First Baptist Church is an impressive structure. Since it was built in 1859, it has undergone several renovations. (Popkin.)

The second church to organize in Northville came about when a Baptist minister arrived in 1833. Four years later, the congregation had raised enough funds to build a permanent church. Remodeled in 1858, the church, located on Wing and Randolph Streets, went through extensive remodeling and updating in the 1950s through 1970s.

The end of the nineteenth century saw the formation of yet another Protestant church in Northville. St. Paul's Evangelical Lutheran Church was formed in 1896. Originally located at Nine Mile and Taft Roads, the small frame building doubled as a school, with the religious services held in German. Only one year later, the cornerstone for a permanent church was laid and a separate schoolhouse was built at its present location on Elm near High Street. The original frame church building was given a facelift in 1930, but was replaced 19 years later by the present brick structure.

Though visiting priests came to Northville as early as the 1880s, a permanent home for Roman Catholic worship was not built until the early twentieth century. On the land where today's Our Lady of Victory Catholic Church stands at Orchard and Thayer Streets, a frame building was constructed in 1922. This serviced the Catholic community for over 30 years, until it was torn down to make room for the current building. The school began in 1952 with only four rooms. Both the church and the school have grown to become among the larger of Northville's religious organizations.

Social changes in the early nineteenth century resulted in a religious awakening in America. While many Protestant churches were experiencing a religious renewal, they were also becoming increasingly active in social causes. As early as the 1790s, the churches of New England had joined together in anti-slavery campaigns. In the early 1800s, they led the way in prison reform, the building of hospitals, schools, and care for orphans, abandoned children, and the handicapped. The churches were also involved in women's education and the founding of female seminaries, which later developed into the first women's colleges.

This strong social conscience and concern for the physical as well as spiritual well-being of man developed into an aggressive missionary program, and the American Missionary Society was formed. This organization employed traveling ministers, such as Reverend Prince, who were instrumental in forming much of Michigan's early religious institutions. The success of the London Missionary Society (LMS) in Asia, however, eventually led to an interest in the possibilities of foreign missions. With the LMS as a major stimulus, secret student societies were formed at Andover Theological Seminary and later at Princeton University. It was in response to requests from these societies that the American Board of Commissioners for Foreign Missions (ABCFM) was formed in 1810 and American foreign missionary work began.

In August 1842, Northville's First Presbyterian Church became authorized to sponsor a mission. It took some time to organize, but in 1873, the Women's Foreign Missionary Society was created in Northville, with Martha Dubuar as its first president. Jennie Dean, a local woman who became a prominent missionary in China for a number of years, ran a school for future missionaries.

According to the *Northville Record*, a resolution was adopted to send Mrs. Dubuar to Fiske Seminary in Persia. Her husband, James, had previously been "educated" in India. The *Northville Record* described the history of the program: "In February 1880, it was decided to do something in the home missionary line and this finally led to the fully organized Home Missionary Society. . . . The Ladies' Aid Society was a long time in existence . . . In 1920 this society and the Women's Missionary Societies were merged into the Women's Union."[12]

Bells were once a vital part of American life. Church bells not only announced weddings, deaths, births, and Sabbath services, they were also responsible for ringing warning signals for the townspeople. America's first church bell was made by Paul Revere in 1792, but it took several years before the quality of the product in America was improved. The country's earliest bells were either salvaged from shipwrecks or manufactured in Europe.

America's most famous bell, the Liberty Bell in Philadelphia, was also made overseas. Since at the time there were no bell-makers in the colonies, an order was sent to England to make a bell. The occasion was the 50th anniversary—or jubilee year—of the William Penn Charter of 1701. The problem came when it was delivered to America. As most schoolchildren already know, the bell cracked on its first ring. Rather than sending it back to England for repairs, local craftsmen were convinced they could handle the job. The bell was re-cast, and rung once more—and again it cracked. Once again it was repaired, and this time it worked. The Liberty Bell rang out for more than 80 years, signaling such noteworthy events as the Battle of Lexington and Concord, the surrender of Cornwallis at Yorktown in 1781, and the death knells of every single signer of the Declaration of Independence, before cracking for its last time in 1935.

In the early part of the twentieth century, Northville's manufacturing district was a thriving, busy area. Furniture, bells, scales, and other items were produced here.

By the mid-1800s, America's bell manufacturing industry had come into its own. Northville eventually became a leader in the manufacture of bells around the turn of the century. The American Bell Foundry Company was formed in 1899, after a fire destroyed one of the town's leading companies, the Globe Furniture Company. It was from the ashes of this fire that the American Bell Foundry Company arose.

Purchasing the newly-constructed Globe company foundry buildings, the bell foundry started out under what the *Northville Record* called "exceedingly auspicious circumstances." Its fame spread rapidly, and in just a few years it was creating products for a worldwide market. The company manufactured bells of all kinds. It also had a general foundry and machine business. It was located as part of an industrial complex at the east end of Cady Street.

By 1902, the *Record* reported, "The fame of the American Bell & Foundry Company's work seems to be rapidly extending into the most untermost [*sic*] parts of the earth. An order has just been received from Egypt for a bell, and letters of inquiry regarding the company's product have recently come from West Africa. The concern is simply overwhelmed with work and although more than thirty men are already employed, more help is needed and will be put on as soon as men can be secured."[13]

Five years later, the company was engaged to create a huge bell closer to home, for St. Paul's Lutheran Church. The bell, which weighed over 1,200 pounds, was dedicated in a special ceremony at the church in 1907.

In 1920, the company was sold to an Ohio firm, and four years later the name was changed to Bell Furnace & Manufacturing Co. After 1924, the company began to phase out its bell-making business. Though by 1931, the business was run strictly as a foundry, bells are still being found all over the country with the inscription, "American Bell Foundry Company, Northville, Michigan."

From their early beginnings in neighborhood homes and barns, both Northville's schools and churches have evolved dramatically over the years. The school system has become one of the nation's best, and the town's religious institutions continue to thrive.

6. WAR

The mid-1800s were a turbulent time in the history of the United States. Like other small towns and big cities alike, Northville was caught up in state and national affairs of the mid-nineteenth century. It came to play an important role in helping slaves escape from the South, as part of the Underground Railroad.

The first rumblings of discontentment in the Southern states were heard as early as the 1830s, and soon the War between the States became imminent. Michigan, as a Northern state, was immediately affected by the Civil War. As a border state with Canada, Michigan—and especially Detroit—became essential in the Underground Railroad, providing escape routes for thousands of runaway slaves. The escape route across the Ohio River into freedom had a very early start. Though there had been slaves in Detroit's earliest days, a law passed in 1787 forbade slavery northwest of the Ohio River. The passing of the Fugitive Slave Act in 1850, which stated that slaves could be arrested in any state for attempting to escape, enraged many Northerners and increased the strength of the anti-slavery movement. Detroit's newspapers of the day called it "that most execrable law that ever disgraced the records of a civilized government."[1] They were proud of Michigan being a free state, and that "neither slavery nor involuntary servitude shall ever be introduced into this State."[2]

The Civil War, according to many contemporaries of that time, was a moral war. It may have been fought in the South, but passions ran high on both sides of the struggle. Redford Township minister Benjamin Sackett, in a letter written to his niece in July 1865, spoke of his sorrow and his pride in the recent war:

> On the part of the North, I consider this a just and unavoidable war. The question resolved into this one point: Shall we have an existence or not, as a nation. If we answer yes, we must fight for it; if no, then farewell liberty, peace, order, nationality, manliness, everything to be held dear by us.
>
> Thank God our Brave Boys said we will defend our country and preserve our freedom . . . and nobly they have done it. We still have a country, a free country,

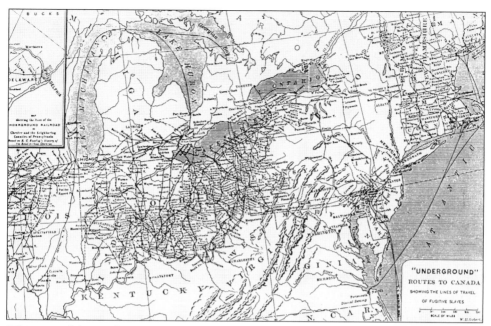

This map of the Underground Railroad lines shows what an integral part of the system Ohio and southern Michigan were in helping the escaped slaves reach freedom.

free from that cursed and abominable Institution of Slavery, which I never could think of without feeling my cheek burn with Shame.[3]

Sackett was not alone in his passion. All during the 1850s and early 1860s, men and women throughout the North risked their safety in adding to the eventual dissolution of slavery. Through a secret system of pathways and surreptitious guides—or conductors—slaves had been led for more than a decade away from their Southern prisons to freedom in the North. Known as the Underground Railroad, this illegal system of travel passed through Michigan before crossing the Detroit or St. Clair Rivers into Canada. Northville took an active, though necessarily subdued, role in these activities. Few records, if any, exist for these secretive times, but folklore has thrived through the years. Songs and stories still tell the tales of the hunted men, women, and children and of the humane owners of houses, sheds, and barns who sheltered them on the road to freedom. Houses still exist that served as hiding places, or "stations" for runaway slaves.

The Underground Railroad was run solely on trust and hope. What the "railroad" actually consisted of was a long line of people—black and white—extending from far into the South all the way up into Michigan and even Canada. This chain was made up of people dedicated to aiding and freeing slaves, providing relief, transportation—in the way of wagons, carts, horses, and mules—food, shelter, and safety all the way into Windsor and beyond.

The system was developed by a Quaker named Levi Coffin, who was known as "the President of the Underground Railroad." The roads and pathways that they ran were

71

nicknamed the "railroad." Stops along the route in Michigan started just above the Southern border, running east and north, including stations in Ann Arbor, Ypsilanti, Farmington, Northville, and Plymouth on the way to Detroit. Stations were generally located within 10 to 20 miles of each other or, roughly, the distance one could walk or ride in a horse-drawn wagon in a day. Travel was done mainly at night, from one station to the next, with the destination ideally reached by daybreak.

Quakers, great exponents of peace and abolition, were instrumental in Michigan's role in the Underground Railroad. Since Farmington had been settled by Quakers, that was a natural place for the "train" to head, but many other communities took up the call for help as well. Nathan Power, son of one of Farmington's original pioneers, was a noted "conductor" on the train, using the Old Quaker Meeting house as a "station." He often accompanied the escaping slaves to Samuel Finney's Hotel in Detroit—their last stop before crossing the river to freedom.

Finney, a prominent Detroiter, was the proprietor of a well-known inn in downtown Detroit, renown throughout lower Michigan by regular guests and escaped slaves as well. During the chaotic Civil War era, Finney's Hotel was often full of guests, many of whom were noted slave-hunters. At the same time, his barn would be crowded with hidden slaves preparing for the last leg of their journey into Canada. That the runaways did in fact escape was indeed a testimonial to the dedication of the "railroad" workers who valued secrecy above all else.

In Northville, a number of places, some still in existence today, once served as stops on the Underground Railroad. One of Northville's oldest buildings is now known as the Cady Inn. Moved to Mill Race Historical Village in 1987, this house was reportedly built

Finney's barn, near his hotel, was located at the northeast corner of State and Griswold Streets in downtown Detroit and served as place of refuge for escaping slaves.

The Cady Inn, built around 1835, was the scene of subterfuge and secrecy during the Civil War, when it served as an Underground Railroad station for escaping slaves. (Popkin.)

in 1835. Until its transfer to the historical village, it stood on Cady Street, where it was said to have been a tavern and—at one time—a station of the Underground Railroad. Another one of the stations in Northville was located near Beck Road and Seven Mile. Originally owned by the Starkweather family, the farm was one of the stops for escapees from the Ypsilanti area in the 1860s. The barn where slaves were hidden stood for nearly a century before being demolished. Other Northville stations were located on the southwest corner of Main and Center Streets, and near what is now Meads Mill Middle School. At the southeast corner of Plymouth and Stark Roads in Livonia once stood a tavern owned by David MacFarlane. This and another building at the corner of Middlebelt and Six Mile served as Livonia's two depots for the Underground Railroad.

Many people escaping from the South found safety here in Michigan, and decided to settle in various communities in the state. Salem Township was one such place where freed slaves chose to settle. Today, a number of Salem residents are descended from these early fugitives.

The Civil War was known by many names. It has been called the War between the States, the War of the Rebellion, the Second Revolution, and more. Most men living in Oakland County joined the 22nd Infantry Regiment of the Michigan Volunteers. This regiment became the largest from the state, with nearly 1,000 men in numerous companies. It was led by Colonel Moses Wisner, former Michigan governor, and it was a proud organization. Mustered into service in August 1862, the 22nd Michigan Volunteer

Infantry was organized at Camp Richardson in Pontiac. A train took the men from Pontiac to Detroit, where they caught a ship headed for Cleveland, Ohio. From there, they took another train and, two days after leaving Pontiac, arrived in Cincinnati. Traveling was exceedingly difficult, especially in the Southern war-torn cities and countryside. One account of the condition of the railroads by a Civil War soldier reported, "The roads were so indescribably bad at this time that the army could make but little progress. I remember it required 36 hours for one train to accomplish the distance of five miles."[4]

In October 1862, the soldiers were sent to winter quarters at Camp Ella Bishop in Lexington, Kentucky. While at Camp Ella Bishop, Private Daniel Herriman, a member of the 22nd Infantry, wrote to his wife, Sarah, about his optimism regarding the conflict (spelling has been corrected for clarity): "I don't think that the war will last longer than spring . . . The rebels look like beggars. We was on the rebels and chased them five days but didn't get set of them . . . In the South flour is 50 dollars a barrel. I think that they can't stand it long."

Despite Private Herriman's optimism, the war was not destined to end any time soon. The winter of 1862–63 was a hard one and conditions at Camp Ella Bishop were severe. Colonel Wisner died in January, a victim of the typhoid fever epidemic raging throughout the camp. On April 1, 1863, the regiment was sent to Nashville, Tennessee, and the 22nd Michigan was now under the command of Lieutenant Colonel William Sanborn. On April 10, Herriman wrote the following of their ordeal:

> We have had a very hard March of it. But we drove the rebels out of the state and
> we took 200 men prisoners and took about 400 head of cattle from them . . . We
> can't tell how heavy their loss was but some of our men went over the ground
> the next day and they said that the rebels was there in piles. They said that they
> was much as 4 or 5 hundred men lost on the ground dead. We did not lose but
> one man.[5]

The regiment fought at the infamous Battle of Chickamauga and in November 1863, at the Battle of Chattanooga at Lookout Mountain and Missionary Ridge, where the Union forces took Tennessee. It took a long time for that final, victorious fight, but the Union troops did prevail. The last action of the 22nd Infantry took place at Atlanta, Georgia, in July 1864. Sixteen officers of the 22nd Michigan Volunteer Infantry were from Oakland County.

The Civil War eliminated slavery in the United States, an institution Benjamin Sackett called "a stain upon our honor as a nation." Though it was fought in the South, which certainly underwent far more visible hardships than the North, neither side would be apt to forget the men from both sides who had fallen.

There are varying accounts of the first Memorial Day, but historians agree that it was the Civil War that inspired it. One account occurred in 1864, when a young woman in a small town in Pennsylvania decorated her father's grave. She made arrangements with another mourner to meet the next year to continue the tradition.

Another story takes place in Mississippi in April 1866, one year after the war ended. Grief-stricken widows paraded to the local cemetery, where they placed flowers on all the

STOCKHOLDERS
OF THE UNDERGROUND
R. R. COMPANY
Hold on to Your Stock!!

The market has an upward tendency. By the express train which arrived this morning at 3 o'clock, fifteen thousand dollars worth of human merchandise, consisting of twenty-nine able-bodied men and women, fresh and sound, from the Carolina and Kentucky plantations, have arrived safe at the depot on the other side, where all our sympathising colonization friends may have an opportunity of expressing their sympathy by bringing forward donations of ploughs, &c., farming utensils, pick axes and hoes, and not old clothes; as these emigrants all can till the soil. N. B.—Stockholders don't forget, the meeting to-day at 2 o'clock at the ferry on the Canada side. All persons desiring to take stock in this prosperous company, be sure to be on hand.   By Order of the
Detroit, April 19, 1853.   **BOARD OF DIRECTORS.**

The allegory of using railroad terminology is evident in this early handbill, dated 1853.

graves, for both the Confederate and Union soldiers alike. In May of the same year, a village in New York reportedly honored the dead in a special ceremony they called "Memorial Day." Later, the U.S. Congress would designate Waterloo, New York, as the "birthplace" of Memorial Day.

In any case, decorating the graves of Civil War soldiers, in the North and the South, led to a special ceremony held in 1868 by the Grand Army of the Republic. It was known as "Decoration Day." The day, which has been celebrated on May 30, or the last Monday of May, ever since, was later officially called "Memorial Day." Celebrations around the country are held annually to honor the hundreds of thousands of men and women who have given their lives to their country.

Detroit's first Memorial—or Decoration—Day celebration took place in 1869. Civil War veterans paraded the streets, and the day was filled with speeches from noted luminaries. Graves all over the city were bedecked with flowers to commemorate the event. Decoration Day in Northville in 1877 was, according to the *Northville Record* of the time, "properly observed . . . business generally being suspended, and all turning out to participate in the festivities of the day." These festivities included a cornet band and distribution of flowers by Union School intermediary students. On May 30, 1878, " as has been customary since the war, [the day] was observed as a sort of a holiday and devoted to the decoration of the graves of the noble army dead," reported the *Record*. "Although the

During the Civil War, most men living in Oakland County joined the 22nd Infantry Regiment of the Michigan Volunteers. A small number of that regiment is seen here.

mortal remains of but a few lie 'neath the sod in our Northville cemetery the remembrance of their heroic struggles and noble sacrifices in defense of home and country, has ever kept their memory green." The next year, Decoration Day was described in the *Record* as the occasion for a "decidedly *high-toned* brass band, whose grand strains made the atmosphere and the souls tremble alike [as it] advanced towards the cemetery."

By the mid-twentieth century, an annual parade was being held in Novi. In 1956, the annual Memorial Day Parade began at the Novi Community Building, marching along Novi Road to the Novi Cemetery, where a Memorial Day address was delivered. Since those post–Civil War days, Memorial Day continues to be celebrated with solemn observances in Northville and Novi. From those few grieving wives, daughters, and sisters in the late nineteenth century, the holiday has remained one of patriotic importance throughout the country.

The memory of the Civil War had barely faded when another conflict brought Americans to stand up for their country. When revolution broke out in Cuba in 1895, it had immediate and adverse effects on the many American investments there. Precarious relations with Spain came to a head in 1898, when a private letter written by the Spanish minister Dupuy deLome was intercepted and subsequently published in the *New York Journal*. The letter was defamatory to U.S. President McKinley, and deLome, unveiled, was forced to resign his position. Then, just one week after the letter's appearance in the paper, another event occurred that would have such disastrous consequences that the United States would once more find itself plunged into another war.

The U.S. Battleship *Maine*, on guard duty at Havana Harbor, was sunk by explosives which killed more than 200 men. "Remember the *Maine*!" became the battle cry, and by

April the country was once again officially at war. Destruction of the Spanish fleet at Santiago on July 3 was an overwhelming victory for America. While over 400 Spaniards lost their lives and 1,750 were taken prisoner, the United States was able to count its casualties on two fingers: one killed, one wounded.

News of the conflict was covered extensively in the *Northville Record*, with detailed accounts in every issue. By July, headlines read, "More Men Needed; General Shafter applies for reinforcements . . . More troops to be sent at once."

Northville boys were quick to answer the call. On July 22, the *Record* listed a number of its citizens who had signed up. "In the present Cuban war Northville is well represented," it wrote. "Besides the present independent military company organized some time ago and which at the present hour has over thirty men drilling and anxious to go to the front, some twenty of the boys have already enlisted."

Three men were assigned to the 32nd Division, stationed at Tampa, Florida; Bert Hill was sent to Santiago with the 33rd; Frank Bovee and Bruce Babcock were both with the 31st at Chickamauga; and the rest were assigned to the 35th Division, stationed at Island Lake.

The lure of the fight was too great for some boys to resist, even if they were a bit too young. One boy, however, managed to find his way to the war, and—luckily—back again. The *Northville Record* ran the following story on July 29:

> A telegram in the *N.Y. Sun* says, "Claude Murdock, the 15-year-old boy who was found in one of the trenches at Santiago, suffering from intermittent fever, is in a far way to recover. Murdock ran away from home and followed the thirty-fourth Michigan boys to Chickamauga. Here he fell in with the men of the Third United States Infantry and went along with them when they were ordered to Cuba.'
>
> "The young man is a son of Jas. D. Murdock, now of Belleville, formerly a resident of Northville.
>
> "[Michigan's 32nd Division was] anchored in Florida for good, but the 31st is preparing to sail for Porto Rico [*sic*]."

"Spain has enough," cried the headlines; "Peace is at hand." The armistice was signed on August 12; the August 19 *Northville Record* described the calm scene in Washington after the war, "The White House, the war department and navy department have resumed their usual quietude, a condition which has not prevailed since the *Maine* was blown up in Havana harbor, Feb. 15. The busy, warlike attitude has entirely disappeared and Washington has settled down to a peace basis."[6] By December, Spain had yielded unconditionally to the offer made by the U.S. government. The Treaty of Paris, signed on December 10, freed Cuba and gave the United States possession of the Philippines, Puerto Rico, and Guam.

The United States emerged from the Spanish-American War as a world power, but winning the war was considered by some historians to be pure luck. A series of ill-planned, poorly conceived circumstances amounted to excruciating hardships for the fighting men. Though Tampa, Florida, was the main point of embarkation for the troops

A number of Northville men served in the Spanish-American War. This is a shot taken on June 20, 1898, of Michigan soldiers landing at Ford Monroe.

going farther south to Cuba, heavy wool uniforms were issued to the unfortunate soldiers. Inadequate supplies—some left over from the Civil War—rotten food, and ancient weapons led to investigations after the war. In fact, most of the casualties of the war came not from enemy fire but from disease and unsanitary conditions. Four Michigan regiments served in the Spanish-American War; those men who returned, including Northville's brave lads, were lucky to survive.

Over the years, Northville men and women would continue to stand up and fight for their county. Their bravery and valor are honored each year at local Memorial Day celebrations, and their courage and dedication are not be forgotten.

7. Business

There were a number of industries in early Northville, but perhaps the most important one in its early years was its first industry, a gristmill. The opening of a gristmill by John Miller around 1826 was what early Northville resident David Clarkson called "the beginning of Northville, and John Miller was the pioneer."[1]

A miller both by name and trade, John Miller constructed one of the first gristmills in the territory. With only two other mills reportedly in existence in the general area at the time, Miller's stone mill served a much-needed purpose for residents of western Wayne County. Previous to the establishment of this mill, area farmers had to travel to Ann Arbor or Pontiac to have their corn or wheat ground into flour.

John Miller began his gristmill sometime between 1825 and 1828, according to various accounts. Located on the site of what is now Mill Race Historical Village, Plymouth Township's first mill was built by neighboring hands, all helping to construct both the building and the dam for the raceway in what was known as a "building bee."

Using a large boulder found a short distance from the site, Miller, along with Israel Nash, a millwright, was able to make up his own burr stones to be used as grinding wheels. Built cheaply, with the machinery made largely of wood, the mill was not as modern as it might have been, but it was efficient and practical. John Miller's mill was a rotary mill, which made use of the rubbing action of the two circular burr stones as the basic principle in grinding the grain.

Miller was a man of firsts. Besides building the first gristmill in Plymouth Township, he was among the earliest to settle in this remote land. He also built the first house in the slowly-developing area. It was a small log cabin and stood on the property near where the mill would soon be built. This first modest little house and its accompanying mill became the major force in creating the tiny town of Northville. From its beginnings in the 1820s, the mill was eventually purchased by Captain William Dunlap, who tore it down in 1847, building a more imposing structure known for many years as the Northville Milling Company, or simply, Northville Mills. By 1889, this company was capable of grinding 1,000 bushels of grain per day.

Northville's first mill was at this site, where the millrace still runs. The site has been memorialized as Mill Race Historical Village. (Popkin.)

Changing technology gradually meant doom for many of the old mills. A new process of grinding wheat was developed in the mid-nineteenth century. By placing the two millstones farther apart, the grain could now be cracked rather than crushed, resulting in a higher-quality white flour. By the late 1800s, metal rollers replaced millstones in many American mills.

Mills of all types and for many purposes were commonplace in the America of 100 years ago. Water-, wind-, and animal-powered mills provided the energy to produce such everyday staples as cornmeal, cider, salt, lumber, plaster, and more. America's first mill was a water-powered device used for grinding corn and nuts. Sawmills existed in New England in the 1600s. The Dutch, who settled in what is now New York State, brought windmills with them, and the idea spread throughout the northeastern coast.

America's earliest mills were, in fact, wind-powered. Dating from 1633, windmills were used as sawmills as well as gristmills for grain. In the Northern states' cold climates, the Dutch-designed windmills were particularly useful as they did not freeze as did those depending on water. David Clarkson described such a scene as follows: "Although the water wheel was enclosed and roofed over, yet in winter the ice would gather on the wheel to such an extent that we had to cut it off, and sometimes the wheel would freeze fast and it had to be cut loose."

Animals were also used, much as a hamster in a squirrel cage, to power various types of household appliances, from butter churns to roasting spits. Dogs were used for smaller chores, while horses on treadmills helped run sawmills.

Water-driven mills relied, of course, on a nearby water source. In Northville, a tributary of the Rouge River became a suitable and convenient source. There were several ways for the water to power the mill. One way relied on the steam's speed to send water under the water wheel. Another was useful in deeper water, where the partially submerged wheel turned from the force of the water. The third and most efficient method was an "overshot" wheel, which turned by the weight of the water going around the wheel. Originally built by the millers themselves, the mills were later constructed by carpenters who specialized in the craft, advertising themselves as "mill-wrights."

Other mills in Northville soon followed Miller's example. In 1890, the Northville Mills was purchased by the Yerkes brothers and became known as the Yerkes Mills. It served the community for nearly 100 years. The Yerkes were able to keep up with the changing technology somewhat by making use of the new, improved process. However, with automation taking over in the early 1900s, which produced flour even more efficiently and of a better, more consistent quality, the old days of the gristmill were definitely numbered. After several owners, the Yerkes Mill was finally destroyed in 1920.

Among the many mills in Northville were the Argo Mills and the Phoenix Mill, both opened in 1837. The Phoenix Mill burned down in 1870, but the Argo Mills operated for 70 years. Sawmills were a common sight in the community, with J.A. Dubuar's

Northville was a mill town in its early years, and the Northville Mills was a major concern. Located on the site of today's Mill Race Historical Village, the Northville Mills was also known as the Yerkes Mills. (NHS.)

81

One of the oldest companies still in business today in Northville is Parmenter's Cider Mill. Begun by Benajah Parmenter in 1873, the mill was opened at its present location on Base Line Road. The mill remained in the Parmenter family until being sold in 1968. Although it is no longer owned by the Parmenters, the name has been retained. Benajah Parmenter is seen here in an early photo working at his mill. (Novi.)

Manufacturing Companies. The Parmenter Cider Mill, still in existence today, was established in 1873. Meads Mill, which today refers only to a middle school in Northville Township, was once a separate hamlet, created by the Mead brothers and formed solely on the basis of a thriving gristmill.

In the early twentieth century, Henry Ford opened what he called "village industries" throughout rural areas in southeastern Michigan to provide farmers with employment during their off-season. According to the *Northville Record*, the " 'village industries' were an attempt to tie the rural areas in with manufacturing."[2] The project began in 1918, when Ford purchased the Nankin Mills. A former gristmill located along the Rouge River just south of Plymouth, the structure was taken over, modernized, and reopened as a factory for engravings, carburetor parts, rivets, and bearings. Ford Motor Company kept the concern going through World War II, when it was taken over by the Wayne County Road Commission. In 1956, it was converted to a nature center as part of Hines Park.[3] When Northville factory owner J.A. Dubuar died, Ford purchased the building and during the winter of 1919, machinery from Ford's Fordson and Highland Park plants were moved to Northville for its subsequent renovation. By March of the next year, the plant began the valve production that would continue for more than half a century. Between 1920 and 1936, over 180 million valves were produced. In 1936, the old structure was replaced by the current building of steel and brick, which is today the home of the Water Wheel Health Club.

The Northville Valve Plant began making intake valves in the 1950s and by the 1960s was involved in producing both intake and exhaust valves. The building was enlarged in 1956 to handle the increased production, and by 1969 the plant employed a staff of 300 who turned out 150,000 valves daily. At that time, it was the last of the village industries still in operation. It provided valves for all the Ford and Mercury cars, with the exception of the Lincoln Continental, until the fall of 1981. With a struggling economy, the plant was forced to shut down and it was eventually sold.

The serene beauty of the park-like grounds, with its expansive lawn and shade trees that frame the gently flowing stream, highlights the main attraction of the site: the waterwheel, which was the symbol for all of Ford's village industry plants. Located on the site of Northville's first mill, the waterwheel is also a symbol for the town—as it turns softly at the side of the building, it is a nostalgic reminder of Northville's first industry.

Other businesses added to Northville's commerce over the years. When Jamestown, Virginia, was settled in 1607, one of the colonists who arrived with the group was a blacksmith. The profession was in such demand that soon there were more blacksmiths in America than almost any other occupation. For more than 300 years, the blacksmith remained among the most significant of the artisans in America.

The name itself refers to the black metal, or iron, that the man would "smite," or hit, with a hammer. A "whitesmith," on the other hand, worked with lighter metals, polishing their works to a high finish, such as bells, fancy locks, and keys.

In a time when most utensils and tools had some form of ironwork attached to them, the blacksmith was perhaps the busiest of his fellow workers. He often doubled in another related profession, such as veterinarian or wagon maker. From forging horseshoes—the job of a "farrier"—to producing fine metalwork such as hinges, guns, wrought-iron tools,

Henry Ford's "village industries" came to Northville in 1920. The Ford Valve Plant operated for nearly half a century. The waterwheel, Ford's symbol of his village industries, is still seen at the side of the building. (Popkin.)

The blacksmith was one of the most important occupations to come to the New World. It remained a vital business in America for centuries. Northville's Hirsch Blacksmith Shop is seen here on Main Street around 1913. (NHS.)

iron tires, padlocks, and more, the blacksmith handled nearly all the items necessary for daily life.

The process of smithing was, by definition, a physically demanding task, requiring great strength and stamina. The workplace began with a hearth, a large fireplace or furnace, designed to withstand immense heat year-round. To maintain an appropriately hot fire, a bellows was connected to the chimney, providing air to keep the fire going nonstop. Generally, an apprentice served much of his time regulating the fire by operating the bellows. By hitting the iron on his anvil, the blacksmith was able to shape the metal into often amazingly intricate works of art.

Though many farmers in the early days had their own forge barns to provide for an emergency horseshoe, the village blacksmith manipulated the more detailed work farmers did not have the talent, or the time, to undertake. The blacksmith was responsible for creating nearly every piece of hardware available in early America, including nails, saws, axes, handles, and pots.

Novi's first industry was a blacksmith shop, opened in 1829 by David Guile. Daniel Johnson was an early Northville blacksmith, who built his shop near the town's first mill. In 1865, John Hisch moved to Northville from New York. Though he also worked as a carriage and wagon manufacturer, he will be known in Northville for years to come as a blacksmith. A reproduction of his stone shop, which stood at the corner of Main and Hutton Streets, may be seen at Mill Race Historical Village. Part of the building currently houses the museum store, but the other half is a working forge, often used by present-day blacksmiths to demonstrate their knowledge of a long-ago craft.

By the late 1800s, Frank N. Perrin ran a carriage manufacturing company, a wagon shop, and a blacksmithing plant in town. According to a promotional booklet about Northville, published in 1892, "Mr. Perrin stands preeminent . . . as a thoroughly reliable shoer of horses . . . Valuable stock is brought from many miles that their shoes may be turned by his expert hand, and his trade is rapidly increasing and extending."[4]

With specialization in later years with gunsmiths, tinsmiths, hingesmiths, and whitesmiths, as well as the Industrial Revolution and mass production techniques of the early twentieth century, the art of blacksmithing began its eventual decline to obscurity. Luckily, historical villages like Mill Race and Greenfield Village have managed to keep this art alive for a whole new generation to appreciate.

In 1874, prominent fish breeder Nelson Clark left his home in Clarkston—which had been named in his honor—for Northville. He arrived with big plans for a state-run fish hatchery. The *Northville Record* wrote of the new venture with enthusiasm: "Nelson W. Clark of Clarkston, the great fish breeder . . . has leased the springs above the village, also the waste water from Ambler's pond, and is to begin breeding salmon, trout [and] whitefish." The hatchery proved to be a gradual success. When Clark died suddenly in 1876, his son Frank assumed control of the fledgling hatchery, turning it into a national leader. In 1880, the business endeavor had grown to become one of the finest fish hatcheries in the country. It was in that year that the United States Government purchased the buildings, making Frank Clark the superintendent of the new U.S. Fish Hatchery, the first federal fish hatchery in the nation.

By the 1890s, the fishery contained about 10,000 stock fish and 250,000 trout of various species. Millions of fish hatched here and were shipped all over the country and the world, from Mexico to Europe and New Zealand. Of the 15 acres it occupied by 1892, a number

When Nelson W. Clark came to Northville in the 1870s, he developed a private fish hatchery. His son, Frank, later leased the concern to the U.S. government, and it grew to become the largest fish propagation station in the world.

The Fish Hatchery was opened around 1875. At the time of its operation, 5 of the 17 acres were under water. This view of the U.S. Fish Hatchery was taken in 1907.

of springs produced about 375 gallons of water per minute. The U.S. Hatchery inspired the creation of a gold fish hatchery on Farmington Road in 1884. Starting with only two pairs of fish, within ten years the prolific couples had produced nearly 10,000 gold fish of numerous varieties.

Frank Clark served as president of the National Fisheries Association before his death in 1910. He was followed by William Thayer, who served as superintendent of the U.S. Fish Hatchery for 20 years. The hatchery lasted well into the twentieth century. By 1935, it was the only federal fish hatchery in Michigan, covering 17 acres, 5 of which were under water. Several buildings were constructed west of Rogers Street along each side of Fairbrook to serve as offices and housing for the hatcheries. Today, the only one of these buildings to remain is the superintendent's cottage, now used as a private home. After the hatchery was closed in the late 1930s, the buildings were destroyed and a park along Fairbrook Avenue was opened. Today known as Fish Hatcheries Park, it is a fitting monument to one of Northville's early industries.

Back in the days of commonplace illiteracy, most shops were identified by visual aids rather than printed signs. A large, somber wooden Indian signified a tobacco shop; a giant boot hanging from a chain denoted a cobbler's shop; a candy-striped pole indicated a barbershop. In another shop of the nineteenth century, one would find green-and-red globes hanging in the window. This was the symbol of a pharmacy: folklore describes the green globe as supposedly indicating the bad (green) blood that went into the store, while the good (red) blood left the store with the prescribed medicine.

Many of the early druggist's medicinal ingredients were extracted from herbs and other natural elements received from pharmaceutical companies like Detroit's Parke-Davis. They were delivered in large tins, and the pharmacist kept the contents in glass jars, stored in a large cabinet behind the counter. On his scales, he weighed the ingredients and, mixing together a specific "recipe" from his prescription books, would combine, smash, and grind up the various substances with his mortar and pestle that he kept conveniently on the counter.

The pharmacy was a vital place for late-nineteenth-century individuals. In fact, most people went to a pharmacist before the doctor when they were ill, relying on the druggist's relatively inexpensive expertise to allay their aches and pains. Pharmacies held an important place in many early communities, including Northville. The Peoples Drug Store was the name of a pharmacy and laboratory in Northville, which opened in 1869. It was run by Dr. C.C. Kingsbury. Another early local druggist was Charles Stevens, whose store was located on Main Street. He held a respected place in the community in the 1890s, with his large stock of drugs and related items. Stevens also produced some of his own medicines, which reportedly sold well and "were recognized as strictly superior," according to an 1892 booklet on Northville.

Many early pharmacies had, along with the prescription counter, a soda fountain or soda bar tended to by a soda jerk, who "jerked" the soda from the taps. Soda bars at the turn of the century generally had marble counters and a mirrored wall, with fancy stools and small tables and chairs.

Ice cream was brought to the Western world by Marco Polo from China; Nero put flavoring into snow, creating the original snowcone; Alexander the Great used snow to cool his drinks. By Dolly Madison's time, ice cream had become the national dessert of

After the U.S. Fish Hatchery was closed, this park was created on its site. Located just outside of Northville city limits, Fish Hatchery Park is a fitting monument to one of Northville's most important industries. (Popkin.)

Fred Sanders was born in Germany, but brought to America his recipes for delectable confectionaries. He also added ice cream, and claimed to have invented the ice cream soda.

the United States. Around 1830, soda water and syrup were added to ice cream, and the ice cream soda was born. Fred Sanders was reportedly the first to bring this innovation to Detroit in 1830. Ten years later, the "unsoda," a soda-less soda was created and called the Sunday Soda. The clergy objected to a treat being named after the sabbath, so the spelling was changed to "sundae," and everyone was happy.

Ice cream cones are another development of this early period of America's sweet tooth. At the St. Louis World's Fair of 1904, on a particularly hot day, the ice cream vendor ran out of dishes. His neighbor, a man selling thin, flat wafers, hit upon a world-shattering idea. He formed his hot wafers into cones and when they cooled they remained in that shape. He offered them to his friend as a substitute for plates. "Cornucopias" were sensational and the name was shortened to "cone" after a couple of years of constant use. Good Humors—ice cream on a stick—were derived in 1929, complete with the white truck and bells that are still popular today.

The combination drugstore/soda fountain lasted well up through the 1960s. Though together they are relics of a past age, individually both the pharmacy and the ice cream shop still hold almost equally important places in today's world. The Northville area is one place that offers world-class ice cream in a relatively small area.

Guernsey Farms Dairy, located on Novi Road near the Novi/Northville border, has been operating in the area for over half a century. It received national recognition in 1984, when its smooth, nutty butter pecan ice cream won fifth place in a *People Magazine* best flavors contest. Originally known as the Red Rose Dairy, located on Center Street in Northville, the company changed its name to reflect the type of cows from which the dairy products derived. The McGuire family of Northville has controlled the business since 1945, one of the few remaining family-run dairies in the state.

Northville was considered to be "ideal dairy country" in the late 1800s. *Northville: The Ideal Suburban Village*, published in 1892, reported that the Northville farms were stocked "with the best cows—sown entirely with sweet clover and watered by pure running springs." The area continued to excel in the dairy business, even up to the twentieth century. By 1931, the *Northville Record* reported that "Four dairies are [a] community asset." They included "Werve's on Beck Road, the Red Rose dairy at the corner of Cady and South Center streets, the Lloyd Morse dairy at the corner of Dunlap and North Center streets and the Northville Creamery, run by Don Miller, on Six Mile Road. All four dairies give delivery service, the Red Rose in Detroit, and the other three in Northville."[5]

In connection with these dairies was a Northville manufacturing company that provided the butter churns for these companies. Butter supposedly got its start centuries ago in a desert in the Mideast. While a horseback rider carried a goat-skin bag of rich milk across the desert, he found to his surprise that the bumpy ride, combined with the heat, had turned his liquid milk to creamy butter. It may not have quenched his thirst, but it did satisfy other tastes, and the discovery became an instant ancient hit.

Butter is made from cream that is skimmed off from the top of the milk. In early days, the cream was poured into a skin bag and swung back and forth to separate the fat. In later years, an earthenware churn was used with a rocking motion to produce the butter. Finally, an inventor took the earlier churn and added a wooden plunger, or dasher, to speed up the process.

Guernsey Farms Dairy, owned by the McGuire family since 1945, has been at its present location on Novi Road in Northville since 1965. (Popkin.)

The country's first butter factory was established in 1856 by R.S. Woodhull of New York. A few years earlier he had created one of the first commercial creameries in the United States. In Northville, the Superior Churn and Manufacturing Company, located on E. Cady Street and run by Fred VanAtta, was reportedly one of Northville's "pioneer manufacturing organizations." "Not only does the Superior Churn company send its products to every state in the union," boasted the *Northville Record*, "but also to several foreign countries, particularly Canada, Scotland and South America." The Superior Churn Company produced more than butter churns as noted in the following: "The chief products of the Superior Company are the Sanitary Churn, Corn Cutter and Sanitary Mixer. The latter product is used chiefly in mixing extracts and syrups. The Sanitary Churn is used at the Northville Laboratories while the Werve Creamery uses a Superior Churn."[6]

Another dairy company that had great prominence in Northville was the Clover Pasteurized Milk Company. Located on Fairbrook Avenue, it made use of a spring-fed pond for its production of condensed milk. The pond has long since been filled in, and is now the location of a tree-studded grassy field known as Joe Denton Park.

Milk condensing helped put the commercial milk industry on its feet. The rural area around Northville was once considered to be "an important milk producing community," according to Frank Harmon, who wrote a history of the town, published in the *Northville Record* in 1927. Charles Rogers was the inventor of a milk condensing machine in the early 1830s. His son, also named Charles, built the large white house on Nine Mile Road in Novi in 1929, which was later turned into a restaurant. Harmon believed Rogers's plant to be "the first plant in America, if not in the world, to successfully condense milk and sell it commercially."[7] Opened in 1833, the plant was located at Fairbrook and Eaton Drive.

Through the years in Northville, there existed the Lansing Milk Condensery, the Clover Pasteurizing Company, the Northville Condensing Company, C.T. Rogers & Sons Condensery, and the Oakland Dairy Plant. As part of the Clover Dairy Company, the Rogers milk-condensing plant went through a series of various names of its own. Known alternately as C.T. Rogers & Sons and Rogers Oakland Plant, the division was sold in early 1908 to T.C. Richardson and then–Michigan Governor Fred Warner, a Farmington resident. At the time it was sold, the plant was, according to a 1908 account in the *Northville Record*, "a losing investment."

Beginning with the Clover Condensery, near the fish hatchery, a milk station was located near the railroad depot along Northville Road. When the Northville Condensing Co. was organized, a plant was constructed near the Yerkes Mill on Griswold. "It was not a financial success," stated the *Record*. Yet, when it too was bought by Warner and Richardson, it was "operated by them for some years as the only successful condensing plant in this part of the state."

The Rogers Oakland plant followed, reorganizing itself as the Clover Dairy Co. This plant, under the operation of Warner and Richardson, was reportedly "one of the most complete and modern ones of the kind in the state and the new owners will never endeavor to operate it to its fullest capacity."

Richardson and Warner sold the business in 1922 to the Gordon-Pagel Company. This venture made Northville an important milk-producing center for even longer. According to one source, "During its existence, the company took top rank for milk condensing in the Western hemisphere." By 1931, the Gordon Baking Co., as it came to be called, was producing 100,000 pounds of milk daily for condensing. After going through the condensing process in Northville, the milk was sent by truck to bakeries in Detroit and, via the Michigan Central Railroad, to Chicago. The *Northville Record* proudly claimed, "The Gordon Baking Co. is the only baking company that has its own condensed milk plant and use all the milk for its own bread baking. By doing this we can make the best condensed milk that can be made and as it is all used in our bread it makes the best bread that can be made."[8]

The general store was an American invention. While Europeans went to specific stores for specific items, Americans, who generally lived in more remote areas, found it convenient to shop at one store for all their needs. One of the most important of the numerous household items to be carried by the local general store was groceries. Novi farm families grew their own produce, selling the excess to the city markets, but many Northville town dwellers relied on the fresh fruit, vegetables, eggs, and other items available at the local store. More exotic items than were grown on area farms were found at many groceries. In 1804, the first bananas were shipped from the Caribbean to New York. Coffee was imported by 1816, and oranges and grapefruits, California grapes and pears were available in local markets. Canned goods and even frozen foods, first created by Clarence Birdseye in the 1890s, were also offered in many general stores throughout the country.

Located in Northville's manufacturing district was the Stimpson Scale and Manufacturing Company. This scruffy-looking group is a construction crew on the site. (NHS.)

One of Northville's major industries of the nineteenth and early twentieth centuries was the Globe Furniture Company. Started in 1873 by Charles Harrington and F.R. Beal as the Michigan School Furniture Company, it became the largest manufacturer of school furniture in the world.

In 1869, Scott and Jackson's of Northville advertised their stock of "Drugs, medicines, Paints, Oils, Brushes . . . a choice stock of Tobaccos and Cigars [and] Groceries," among other things. The change from general store to grocery store was gradual, but by the late nineteenth century, local merchants began to specialize, too. Novi's E.E. Goodell started a "traveling grocery store." According to the *Northville Record*, Goodell would buy his groceries at Detroit, "selling them and taking back a load of produce" to Novi in 1877. By 1892, Northville contained a meat market, owned by F.A. Miller, and a grocery store of A.H. Kohler, both proudly noted in a promotional booklet on the town:

> Mr. Kohler has established a wide reputation for honorable dealing and his trade extends to all parts of the county. His stock is fresh, large and complete in every branch of the grocery business. . . . [The quality of Miller's stock], his unremitting attention to the details of the business, and his general qualifications as a genial businessman . . . have tended to the securing of his present large and well-established trade.

F. Thompson & Co. opened a new meat market in town in 1893. A newspaper advertisement exclaimed that the company "is now thoroughly equipped for business. Market newly overhauled, everything new and first class. All kinds of best qualities of fresh and salt meats . . . at lowest market prices."[9]

By the turn of the century, a radical idea known as self-service was instituted in California and the world got its first taste of what would develop into the "supermarket." Clarence Saunders created a turnstile entrance and a regular check-out system in his Piggly-Wiggly self-service grocery store in Memphis, Tennessee, in 1916. The idea was so successful that within seven years, his single Memphis store exploded into a nationwide chain of nearly 3,000 markets. The age of grocery stores had truly arrived. Whereas 150 years ago one could find dry goods, produce, and groceries all under one roof, today's shoppers have the same convention at stores such as Big K-Mart, Meijers, and others. As in other phases of life, the trend has come full circle.

As general stores tended to become more outmoded and specialization started to take place, one store in Northville was still able to cover a number of gift occasions, from books to eyeglasses. Whether it was a pair of "Johnston and Conrath's patent Economical Spectacles," watch repair, or a "2 oz. silver Hunting case watch . . . for $16," A.E. Rockwell Jewelers was the place to be in the Northville of the mid-nineteenth century. From 1868, Rockwell's jewelry store was part of Northville's business scene, continuing for at least 30 years.

Jewelers and clock makers were often synonymous in early America. When the Northville Methodist Church wanted a clock for a new tower in 1893, they turned to A.E. Rockwell. Described by the *Northville Record* as a "four-dial A.S. Hotchkiss, eight-day strike, gravity escapement" product weighing 1,500 pounds, it came from the famed Seth Thomas Clock Company of Connecticut. The donor of the clock remained a mystery for some months before his name was revealed as John Gardner. The *Record* proclaimed, "all

This early view of the Northville Methodist Church shows the prominent clock tower; the clock was donated by John Gardner in 1893.

Northville is sounding the praises of 'the grand old man.' Singular as it may seem there are men in Northville who kick on this magnificent gift, because the striking of the clock will tell their wives the hour they get in nights."[10] Despite the misgivings of a few Northville residents, most were appreciative of Gardner's generous gift. In fact, Rockwell's clock atop the church steeple became a village icon, and when it would, on occasion, stop working, it was time for concern, as this February 1929 *Northville Record* article attests,

> Tick, Tock, Tick, Tock. But there was no Tick Tock for several days during the biting cold weather.
>   Sleet, wind and ice broke the western face of the clock in the church steeple on the Methodist church and for something like three or four days the village clock didn't tick or tock.[11]

A similar time-stopping event had happened earlier, at the turn of the century, "to the same clock . . . for the same reason." Both times, workmen were sent to repair the damage, and the clock was returned to working order in a timely fashion.

The earliest clocks in our country came with the Dutch and English settlers in the seventeenth century. Though in previous centuries household clocks were considered luxuries, by the 1800s they were being commercially developed and reasonably priced for all homes. Connecticut, in particular, became a noted clock-making center. In 1900, one could purchase a "Celebrated Parker Alarm Clock" made in Meridian, Connecticut, from Sears for $1.20.

Mr. Rockwell himself was considered to be in demand as a watchmaker, reportedly sought after by customers throughout the area for his fine workmanship. He was also a practiced optician who prided himself on his low prices, as evidenced by his ad in an 1877 issue of the *Northville Record*: "To my Plymouth, Northville and all other patrons. I have not issued a price list on work as some others have. I will do all watch and clock work as cheap as it can be done anywhere—quality considered." By the turn of the century, Rockwell would have some competition in keeping those prices low. When Sears, Roebuck & Co. issued the first mail-order catalog in 1891, they brought inexpensive, convenient items directly to the home. By the fall of 1900, the *Sears, Roebuck and Company Consumers Guide* was noted as the "Cheapest supply house on earth."

While Mr. Rockwell may not have listed his prices, Sears boldly advertised gold-filled spectacles, "warranted 10 years," for $1.90. The catalog itself even provided an eye test chart, and one could get "riding bow spectacles" for as low as 75¢, "fine crystalline lenses" included. Gold-filled rings or sterling silver bracelets were available from the Sears catalog for well under $1. If that were not enough, the *Kresge's Katalog* of 1913 offered not only a money-back guarantee on all items, but it also promised "nothing over 10 cents" throughout the store, thus giving Sears some tough competition. Though you might not be able to buy eyeglasses through the Kresge catalog, you could find a ring to rival that of Rockwell's or Sears for one thin dime.

Rockwell sold more than just jewelry. He included with his stock such items as school and art supplies, books, and stationery. But he was no match for the huge supply houses like Sears or Kresge's, where one could buy anything including—in Sears's case, at least—the kitchen sink.

From about 1890 through 1940, certain house builders in America gained prominence from what was believed to be an unusual product: houses by mail. More homes were built during this era than in all of the country's previous history, but prefabricated homes were by no means unique to the twentieth century. In fact, as early as 1820, when the first missionaries sailed to the Hawaiian Islands, a prefabricated house followed, to be constructed a year later. This durable New England–style saltbox still stands in Honolulu as Hawaii's oldest structure.

By the 1890s, the prefabricated house was a regular phenomenon in America. Just after the turn of the century, an added convenience was provided: mail-order catalogs. For the first time, one could choose a house from a catalog and have it sent by train—usually in two boxcars—almost to the site. A book about the Sears mail-order homes, *Houses by Mail*, claims that catalog houses eliminated the need for an architect and builder. Most homeowners need only to hire someone to put the pieces together. This kept costs down considerably, and the houses were popular, well-built, quality structures. Of the six major catalog-house companies to supply pre-cut, conventional balloon-frame houses throughout the United States, three of them were located in Michigan alone. According to *America's Favorite Homes*, a book by Robert Schweitzer and Michael Davis, the forerunner of these catalog-house companies was the Aladdin Company of Bay City.

Perhaps the most well-known of these companies, however, was Sears. Sears came out with its first mail-order catalog for houses, called *Book of Modern Homes and Building Plans*,

This is a sample of a typical bungalow from Northville's Grand River Lumber and Coal Company's 1929 catalog. This model and other houses listed in the book may be seen throughout the city. (Popkin.)

Northville's Grand River Lumber and Coal Company issued catalogs for mail-order houses from 1902 to the 1930s. (Popkin.)

GRAND RIVER LUMBER and COAL CO.

Build a Home First

Northville 30   NORTHVILLE, MICH.

in 1908. Sears's *Modern Homes* popped up all over the country. Many that were built in Michigan, from Grand Rapids to Ann Arbor, are still in use. So many were built in Detroit, in fact, that an attractive one-story house in the 1931–1933 catalogs was known as "the Detroit." Another style, "the Lewiston," dating from 1929 to 1939, was constructed in Farmington. The two-story, five-bedroom house ranged in price from $1,527 to $2,037 in the catalog.

Though Sears may have led the pack, other businesses produced their own smaller catalogs. Local lumberyards also issued house catalogs, or "plan books." Catalog-house expert Michael Davis explained that these generic plan books were "widely distributed in the 1930s by a Minneapolis company called National Plan Service. These plans were sold to local lumberyards around the country with local imprints on the cover. A customer would then order the plans [and of course the building materials] from the lumberyard."[12]

Northville's Grand River Lumber and Coal Company, managed by W.R. Seyfang from 1902 to the early 1930s, issued one such catalog. Their 1929 plan book featured plans for over 80 homes, many of which may be seen along Northville city streets today.

Clothing was also available at many of the mail-order houses, though fashions changed rapidly over the years. When schoolchildren visit Northville's Mill Race Historical Village on school outings, they get the chance to spend a day in the past. Besides reading out of reproduction McGuffey Readers and sitting at old-fashioned desks in a nineteenth-century one-room schoolhouse, they also have the opportunity to dress up a bit like their nineteenth-century counterparts. Girls can choose from a variety of pinafores and bonnets, while boys may select a natty vest to wear over their T-shirts.

When Northville and Novi were first settled in 1825, men were just beginning to wear long pants. Previously, knee-breeches had been popular, but this fashion went out of style only to return 100 years later in the "knickerbocker" style of the 1920s. Ladies who stepped off the boats in Detroit's harbor in 1825 generally wore long, high-waisted dresses with "leg-of-mutton" sleeves that puffed out from the shoulder to the elbow and narrowed from elbow to wrist. High beaver hats were worn by men, encouraging the exploration of western lands—such as Michigan—to capture these valuable animals.

In 1830, the first woman's magazine was founded and women even in rural areas like Novi could see first-hand what was being worn in the fashion centers of the world. *Godey's Lady's Book* set the pace for women's fashions for nearly 70 years. Children in early Northville and Novi often looked like miniatures of their parents. Girls wore wide-skirted, fussy dresses, while boys frolicked in either long smock-like jackets known as tunics or in short, tight jackets, which were popular as the "Eton" jacket, over long, tight pants.

By the 1850s, Amelia Jenks Bloomer tried to encourage reform for women by introducing full pantaloons worn underneath a shorter skirt. "Bloomers" were treated with ridicule and amusement, but the practicality of the garment eventually overcame the scorn.

Though most garments needed to be made at home, by the mid-nineteenth century, new inventions began to change the look of fashion. At the same time Amelia's bloomers hit the population, a Boston inventor named Isaac Merritt Singer came out with a domestic sewing machine able to be used by the average housewife. It was a sensation. To purchase the newfangled object in Northville, one merely had to go to the doctor. Dr. J.M. Swift acted as an agent for a self-threading shuttle sewing machine in the late 1870s.

Making up patterns, however, could be time-consuming, and at least one local entrepreneur took advantage of the by-now common household appliance. "Have you a sewing machine?" asked a *Northville Record* advertisement of 1893. J.R. Doelfs announced that he would be in Northville for two weeks in August, ready to "Cut paper patterns for anyone for suits, pants or overcoats, after the latest New York styles . . . at reasonable prices, so you can cut and make your own garments."

Local tailors also advertised, such as F.J. Hoar and Mary Phillips, who advertised dressmaking for Northville's ladies desirous of fashionable styles in 1876. In 1896, Bruno Fredyl came to Northville and opened a tailor shop. His small one-room establishment grew over the years to become one of Northville's major businesses for nearly 100 years, before it closed in 1992. Styles may have changed over the years, but fashion has always been essential to daily life.

Before malls, downtown Northville used to be the place to shop. In 1957, downtown merchants tried a "crazy idea" and kept their stores open all night. Opening on midnight in May 1957, all the shops in town turned up their lights and dropped their prices for an all-night "Sell-a-thon." Announcements of the all-night sale were made before a number of races at Northville Downs Racetrack in an attempt to encourage out-of-towners to shop and get to know the town. Prices were dropped up to 40 percent in the various

MAIN STREET, NORTHVILLE, MICH.

Horse-drawn buggies vied with the interurban streetcar on Northville's Main Street in 1908. In the early part of the twentieth century, Main Street served as one of the main shopping districts of Northville.

clothing, hardware, jewelry, gift, and other shops along Main and Center Streets that night. The sale brought in many shoppers looking for bargains and proved to be a great success.

The sweet smell of vanilla pervades the air at certain times of the year, as one passes along Fairbrook Drive in Northville. For more than eight decades, the rich fragrances from the Northville Laboratories have scented the surrounding neighborhood. The laboratory was started in 1915 by E.C. Langfield and his son, Conrad E. They began the manufacture of flavoring, extracts, and drug specialties. By pioneering a new distillation process, the company quickly became prominent in the field. It remained a family business for many years. In 1931, C.E. Langfield, a pharmaceutical chemist formerly with Detroit's Parke-Davis Company, was president of the company. His father, an engineer, served as vice-president and owner. Before the elder Langfield died in 1936, he sold the laboratory to his son. In 1991, Jogue Incorporated, a full-service flavor company based in Detroit, acquired the laboratory. They continue to manufacture dairy ice cream flavors, extracts, and toppings in Northville under the old Northville Laboratory name. The main feature of the Northville Labs was and still is vanilla extracts.

Vanilla flavoring first became popular when Queen Elizabeth I had occasion to sample it with pleasing results. Her royal apothecary extolled its virtues as having healing properties, and the flavor became an exclusive luxury for the upper classes. Originally found only in Mexico, vanilla beans have since been successfully grown in other countries around the world, from Indonesia to Tahiti to Madagascar. Vanilla beans come from a flower of the orchid family. A 1935 article in the *Detroit Times* described the process of obtaining vanilla extract:

> The pods or beans, as they are generally called, are shipped here in tin boxes. They are carefully selected, chopped, and blended into various combinations. The chopping is done by placing the beans on a maple block and bringing vertical knives down. This method is preferred to grinding because it does not set up heat, which is said to destroy delicate flavoring aldehydes, according to C.E. Langfield, president of the Northville Labs.
>
> Next the chopped beans are placed in a large tank which is nothing more than a vacuum percolator. A solvent of pure alcohol and fine spring water, for which Northville is famous, is used. Percolation is achieved by a pressure vacuum circulation of the solvent through the chopped vanilla beans for about forty hours. Percolation usually takes place at room temperature. Two or four-fold extracts are made by merely increasing the quality of the beans, but beyond the four-fold point vanilla makers struck a snag—they had reached the saturation point.
>
> Here, Langfield went one step further and adopted the distilling process. The vanilla extract could not be boiled because the flavor and aroma would be lost, so it is boiled under pressure and the temperature never reaches an injurious point.[13]

In the 1930s, the Northville Labs were the suppliers of flavors for local ice cream manufacturers such as the Detroit Creamery and Arctic Dairy Products Company of Detroit. Sanders Company was another major customer "which uses Northville extracts exclusively both in ice cream and in baked goods." By 1935, the Northville Labs reportedly ranked as one of the six largest vanilla extract producers in the country. Its products were shipped all over the United States and to Cuba. The *Detroit Times* explained, "The company is known not only for the quality of its products but because the extracts are not only percolated in glass lined tanks but also stored in glass lined containers, which protects the flavor."[14] Quality and dependability were important factors to the labs and "Despite the excellence of Northville water," the *Northville Record* assured, "the Northville Laboratories doubly assures the purity of their products by distilling all water used for compounding purposes."

The labs deduced that the best taste came from combining 30 to 40 different types of beans, along with 100 miscellaneous flavoring extracts. Today the company advertises three categories of vanilla: Bourbon, Bali Indonesian, Mexican, and Tahitian-type blends; pure vanilla from various blends; and natural and artificial vanilla in what the company's brochure calls the "finest blends that produce a true vanilla taste." The scented air in the neighborhood near the Northville Labs gives away its appropriate address: 1 Vanilla Lane.

The demise of many old Northville businesses in recent years is a sad occurrence, but it is nothing new. In 1927, the oldest business in Northville was torn down to make way for two large new stores. An old frame structure on Center Street had been built as a drugstore around 1867. First run by Asa M. Randolph, it was located next to the old post office, before the latter moved to the Lapham Bank Building. In April 1931, yet another old Northville landmark bit the dust. The *Detroit Free Press* explained as follows in April 1931:

> The building once known as "Hungerford's General Store," is falling prey this week to the hammers, picks and crowbars of a wrecking crew . . . while it is being razed to make way for a modern business building, oldtimers recall days when the general store was one of the most modern structures in town.
>
> Built by John B. Hungerford in 1831, this store was the center of civic activities and social events of the community for many years. During these early days, Northville was a village of less than 100 inhabitants . . .
>
> It was in this upstairs room that the first Masonic Lodge of Northville was formed . . .
>
> Late in the '60s, "ready-made" clothes and bustles were introduced into the old Hungerford store, which changed its name to the "Hungerford Emporium" . . .
>
> When the wrecking crew tore down the foundation of the building, they found that the huge hand-hewn beams had been fastened together with wooden pegs, eight inches long and about one inch in diameter.
>
> The new building, which will occupy the site of the old, will house the *Northville Record*, and have several additional offices.
>
> Some day in early July the building will be opened with ceremonies, and the new building will be dedicated just 100 years after Mr. Hungerford completed his general store, and opened his business place, the finest in the town. And now, as the old hand-hewn structure falls under the blows of the wrecking crew, the ring of the steel on the hardwood tolls the knell of a past generation.[15]

Though many residents may have been distraught at the loss of such a historic site, Northville's oldest resident in 1931, Charles Sessions, was philosophical about it. Interviewed by the *Free Press*, Sessions "was asked if he regretted the passing of the old familiar landmarks, and he said, 'No, I don't dislike to see the changes, as long as I know they will benefit the community as a whole, better than the old things did. Take this building, for instance. The old Hungerford building had done a lot of good and was useful to the community for almost a hundred years. It's time there was a change.' "[16] Many changes have indeed occurred in Northville, making it go from a struggling milltown to a trendy, modern suburb.

8. COMMUNICATION

The idea of sending letters from one person to another is an ancient one. The forerunner of the modern postal system began as early as 550 B.C. in Persia, and the innovation spread quickly throughout the world. By the fifteenth century, government-owned postal systems were established throughout Europe. Two hundreds years later, these ideas came with the colonists to America. Though at the time there was not much call for an inland mail service within the colonies—as they tended to keep pretty much to themselves—there was a good deal of service needed for letters coming to and from friends and relatives across the sea. Eventually, postal service between the colonies became necessary. By the 1700s, most roads were created specifically for couriers who would travel from one city to another with the express purpose of delivering mail. Benjamin Franklin, as the colonies' first postmaster, helped to expedite and improve this service. Following the Revolutionary War, the establishment of post offices and post roads was included in the Constitution.

Northville pioneer David Clarkson described this early procedure in his memoirs:

> The principal mail route in the [Michigan] Territory was from Detroit to Chicago . . . The mails were put into small leather bags and securely locked with large iron padlocks; each postmaster had a key. The Michigan Stage Company had the contract to carry the mails. They used large heavy coaches, hung on leather springs with a seat in front on the outside for the driver and the mail bags, and a large boot behind for the trunks, and seats inside for eight to twelve passengers. They were drawn by four horses.
>
> Whenever the stage approached a post office the driver would blow a tin horn, so as to give notice of his coming. He would drive up to the post office, throw out the bags which the postmaster would take in and unlock, empty out on the floor or table, sort out what was directed to his office, place the rest back in the bag, lock it securely and throw it back to the driver. No driver, or other person was allowed to handle the mails, without first being sworn to support the Constitution of the United States.[1]

Mail delivery has come a long way. This early motorized vehicle was part of the Detroit Postal Service in the early 1900s.

Though used in Europe since the 1600s, the postage stamp wasn't adopted by the United States until the 1840s and introduced to Detroit in 1847. Prior to that time, it was the recipient of the letter who paid the postage rather than the sender.

According to Clarkson, "At first the postage on letters ranged from 6¢ to 25¢ according to distance and it was not required to be prepaid. Those that received letters then had to pay the postage, and the postmaster frequently trusted those who received letters for their postage."

Mail arrived in Northville from Detroit once a week. Northville's post office was founded in 1831, with J.M. Mead as the first postmaster. He served in this position for eight years before building a flour mill with his brother and creating a town of their own—and a post office—known as Meads Mills.

In the early 1800s it took up to a month or more to get a letter from New York or Boston—former homes of many of the early area settlers—and the month-long wait to hear from relatives and friends was undoubtedly a trying one. By the 1870s, the delivery of a letter from the east took only 48 hours.

In the mid-fifteenth century, an invention which changed the world was partly responsible for the books and newspapers one reads today. Johann Gutenberg, a German printer, has been acknowledged as the inventor of moveable type. This extraordinary innovation made printing quicker and easier, thus enabling the publication of more and more materials. The success of Gutenberg's press was felt throughout Europe, and by 1539 a printing press was set up in what is now Mexico. Printing enabled newspapers to spread news of current events, books to teach children, and Bibles to pass along the word of religion all over the world.

Over the years, improvements in printing continued, with a hand press developed in Pennsylvania in 1816, a rotary printing press invented in 1846, and the web press—which printed out on a web or roll or papers—which came out in the late 1800s. The printing press was essential for early American settlements along the East Coast and later in the Northwest Territories, of which Michigan was once a part. Keeping in touch with other settlers, as well as providing necessary contact with the outside world, was vital to these pioneers.

Freedom of the press was integral to these early newspapers, and an important part of the founding of this country. Erastus Ingersoll, Novi's first settler, was one of those who believed strongly in the freedom of the press, as well as the integrity of the writers. He kept in contact with other early settlers, such as John Allen. Allen was one of the first to settle in what became Ann Arbor, named in part after Allen's wife.

Allen had been able to obtain a printing press early in the life of the community and began a newspaper in Washtenaw County that reached across the boundaries to Ingersoll in Oakland County. In a letter written to Allen on Christmas Eve, 1829, Ingersoll congratulated his friend on acquiring the press. He wrote fervently of his beliefs:

> If the press is under any restraint save a firm regard to truth and honesty, I do consider it, instead of a blessing, a scourge and a judgment upon the law, for since our government is in the hands of the people, and all the officers amenable to them, and the press the medium through which we mostly obtain information . . . the responsibility of the press must be great.[2]

Many area newspapers began in the nineteenth century. The *Northville Record*, which began in 1869 as the *Wayne County Record*, is the oldest continuing weekly newspaper in Wayne County. The paper was actually printed in Detroit when it first began, at the offices of the *Detroit Free Press*. The four-page paper was issued twice a month and included local gossip, many ads, and a smattering of state and world events.

Despite editor Samuel Little's claim that "there's nothing in a name," when the paper changed its name to the *Northville Record*, it was cause for celebration in the small town. Less than a year after it had begun, editor Little proudly boasted the arrival of their own press, as well as changes in format. In the fall of 1870, the *Record* offices were moved to a "more central location and a more convenient apartment on Main Street."

With the arrival of the new "Hoe" printing press came also a change in style. Another column was added to make a six-column page, which Little considered to be a more "respectable sized paper, comparing favorably with many journals of years standing." Paid advertisements often took up most of the printed space, and were usually given page one coverage.

Early newspapers like the *Northville Record* were sold by subscription, not by individual copy. There were no corner newsstands in the early 1800s, and the paper survived by its ads and its subscribers. Sam Little pleaded regularly with his readers and admonished those who ignored the importance of his paper. He lamented the following regarding some of the local firms:

> [who] have failed to give our paper any support in the way of advertising, thus showing little or no regard for its rise, or downfall. We hope that they may turn over a new leaf and lend a hand in sustaining their local paper, for the ensuing year. . . . It takes a smart town to keep up a paper, and wherever a local paper is issued regularly, having an income that will make it a permanent institution, that town may justly consider itself smart, in every sense of the term.

Little went on to thank his subscribers, vowing to "try to publish a still better paper."[3]

With incredible changes taking place daily in the United States after the Civil War, there was never a lack for news, and more and more papers flourished at this time. It was estimated that, by the end of the Civil War, one out of every 12 Americans read a newspaper. Thirty years later, one out of nine people in this country were habitually reading a paper.

Reconstruction in the South and the Industrial Revolution in the North made for a wealth of advancements in the middle of the nineteenth century. News of new inventions and technological achievements continually made headlines in newspapers around the country. In addition to major events of the day, newspapers of the time—including the *Northville Record*—featured a serialized romance of a multi-chaptered travelog prominently among its articles, often starting on page one.

Samuel H. Little remained editor of the paper for nearly 30 years, seeing it go from a struggling semi-monthly to the weekly it has been ever since. Freedom and honesty of the press is as important today as when Erastus Ingersoll wrote, "Our peace and prosperity rest on the virtue and integrity of the press."

Another way of reaching one's neighbors came to Northville in the 1870s. When the United States was celebrating its centennial in 1876, an amazing voice-throwing contraption was invented by Alexander Graham Bell in Boston, Massachusetts. Bell called it the telephone, but it was regarded as a plaything by most people at first. After a few years, businesses throughout the country began to see the usefulness of such an object, and by 1879, there were telephone companies throughout the country, ranging as far away as Honolulu, Hawaii.

The telephone came to Detroit directly from the inventor. Two officials of the American Detroit Telephone Company contacted Bell for permission to bring the telephone to Detroit. Bell assigned his father-in-law, Gardiner G. Hubbard, as his agent, and in March 1877, the phones were delivered.

Like the many disbelievers when man first walked on the moon, Detroiters of those early years also tended toward skepticism. Many listeners at an early demonstration were convinced that the voice they heard came not from several miles away, but from someone shouting through a tube from an upper floor in the same building.

Thomas Watson, Bell's chief assistant who had actually built the first telephone, paid a visit to Detroit in 1878, representing the nationwide Bell Telephone Association. His visit helped promote the success of the instrument even further to Detroiters. That year, the first telephone exchange was created in Detroit, with 6 miles of wire and 20 subscribers. Only six months later, a directory was published, listing over 100 new customers.

The telephone came to Northville in 1883, with the first telephone exchange located at the grocery store of B.A. Wheeler. With 100 telephone lines, it was operated by a single switchboard operator. The first lines were used by local businesses only, before moving to residences as well. Gradually, service was extended, and Northville was lucky enough to fall between the first long distance line between Detroit and Holly.

The Michigan Telephone Company in Detroit grew rapidly, to nearly 8,000 miles of wire in 1896. Almost 5,000 telephones were in service by the turn of the century. Independent phone companies abounded. By 1897, the Northville Telephone Company extended its wires to Novi, with its central offices in E.C. Goodell's General Store. Other Novi customers on the line included the Whipple Lumber Company, Warner's Cheese Factory, and the residences of George and W.A. Whipple.

Warner and Whipple soon formed yet another independent company, thus creating a widespread dispute between the two local firms. On March 4, 1898, the situation exploded and the *Northville Record* reported on the dissension: "The directors of the Northville Telephone company were red-headed Wednesday morning when it was learned that George Whipple, of the Warner-Whipple Telephone company had cut the

The telephone poles lining Main Street are a sign of the future of communication in this 1910 view of Northville.

These telephone repairmen are seen in Detroit near the turn of the twentieth century, when telephone service was still in its infancy.

Northville Co.'s wire near the Whipple Lumber Co.'s offices at Novi. The Northville Co. says it is a piece of spite work as a most contemptible trick."

Whipple reportedly wanted as many subscribers on his line as possible, despite the fact that his company was already over-burdened with customers. The paper was clearly on the side of the Northville company, and declared that Warner was neither a part of "the wire-cutting act or that he even knew that it was to be done."[4]

By the turn of the century, the various telephone companies decided to join forces and 1913 saw the end of duplicate telephone service in Northville. The Michigan State Telephone Company moved its equipment into the Lapham Bank Building, occupying offices of one of the former independent companies. The consolidation brought about improved service and happy subscribers.

Direct dialing—something taken for granted today—did not reach Northville until the summer of 1958. Previously, all calls had to go through the local operator. At the time of its installation, the *Northville Record* marveled at the rapid progress the telephone system was taking. "In the span of five years," they wrote in awe, "Northville has seen the earliest and the latest in telephony."[5]

Freedom of speech and press are essential components of democracy. Communication of such freedoms—by mail, through newspapers, or over telephone wires—is vital for such democracy to exist. Without this freedom, as Erastus Ingersoll so heatedly wrote, there would arise "a scourge and a judgment upon the law."

9. Sports and Recreation

Ragtime, baseball, rocking chairs, and fortune-telling were among the popular pastimes of Americans at the end of the nineteenth century. But the most prevalent fad of all was "Bicycle Fever."

The first bicycle was invented in England in 1839. Known as a "velocipede," it was quite dissimilar to the low-slung handlebars and multi-geared vehicles today's riders are accustomed to seeing. The iron-tired wheels differed in size, with the front tire a full 10 inches smaller than the one in the back. Despite its unusual appearance, the contraption gained swift popularity. This was, after all, the first vehicle to move faster on the roads than a horse. By 1861, a French coach builder became the first unexpected manufacturer of an odd-looking bicycle, and the invention was on its way. Great Britain saw its first production models for sale in 1869 as French imports, and the items soon came to America.

In 1872, the most popular bicycle was the "Ordinary," with its high front wheel and small rear wheel. This style prevailed for the next 13 years. The 1870s saw many improvements, including the rear-wheel-driven "safety" bicycle. The bicycle-making industry began in the United States with the Pope Manufacturing Co. of Boston in 1877.

The craze continued with further advancements in the next decade. The year 1885 saw the most drastic change in style, with the British safety bicycle that featured two low wheels of equal size. This style was introduced in the United States four years later. The next major improvement was made by John Dunlop, of Belfast, Ireland, who created the pneumatic tire in 1888. Dunlop's Pneumatic Tyre Company was quick to prosper, and by 1891, the company was turning out some 3,000 tires a week. This feature did the trick for boosting an already popular sport to unlimited heights.

The *Northville Record* of those years is filled with ads boasting the superiority of the pneumatic tire. In those days, the name "Victor" was synonymous with bicycle—not unlike the name of Schwinn today. Victor bicycles were manufactured by the Overman Wheel Co. of Boston, and the Victor "Flyer" of 1893 was a sleek, streamlined model.

The Detroit Wheelmen's Club, which was headquartered in this impressive three-story house in 1891, boasted a membership of 175 members.

Bicycle fever hit the Northville area around 1893. Not an issue of the paper went by without an ad for Victor bicycles. Interestingly, though the area has at least three bicycle shops today, the only local place to buy them during the bicycle's heyday was at Sands & Porter, a furniture store and funeral parlor. Located at 72 Center Street in Northville, they were the first to act as local agents for the Overman Wheel Co.

As roads continued to improve, cyclists continued to increase. In 1891, the *Detroit News* estimated the city as having about 800 "wheelmen," and bicycle clubs abounded. In Detroit alone were the Detroit Wheelmen's Club, with 175 members and a three-story clubhouse; the Business Men's Bicycle Club; the Wolverine Boys' Club; and an informal women's group. The Northville Wheelmen's Club included both men and women in its organization. Most of the cycling groups belonged to the National League of American Wheelmen, and the Northville/Novi area was no exception.

In 1893, a group of about 25 cyclists were reported to make an excursion from Novi to Island Lake. The *Northville Record* stated, "The continually increasing number of these vehicles seen on the roads indicates that [either] that manner of locomotion is becoming more and more popular, or that the wheels are becoming cheaper."[1] Whichever the case, by 1900, there were more than 10,000,000 bicycles in the United States. The most popular song was "Bicycle Built for Two," and it was only when improved roads brought automobiles to the forefront did "Bicycle Fever" finally take second place in the American passion for transportation.

Despite the popularity of bicycles throughout the nation, there were still some who thought the sport should be confined to men. The *Northville Record* was clearly not of this opinion, as can be seen in the following story written in 1893 about prominent American lawyer and social leader Ward McAllister and his strident views on the subject:

> Ward McAllister permits American young women to ride tricycles because the Princess of Wales and her daughters ride tricycles. But it "is highly improper," quoth Wardie, "for young women to use bicycles." Dear! dear! A woman mounted upon a tricycle looks like a spider, it is true, and she can make no sort of speed. Likewise the tricycle is fatiguing to operate; moreover, it is rather apt soon to make a creaking noise that sets sensitive nerves crazy. But if the Princess of Wales is willing to wear herself out and look like a spider and not cover any distance worth speaking of besides, of course that settles it. But if some of our modest, merry, pretty American women who, with the full approval of their parents, husbands or grandmothers and without a thought of impropriety, flit gracefully through our city parks every day upon bicycles, occasionally taking long and health bringing tours in the same manner, get hold of Wardie McAllister we wouldn't take even chances on him. They would tell him, these independent American girls, that immodesty exists in his own toadish little mind and nowhere else. If the Princess of Wales were to ride a bicycle, appearing just once upon it, Ward McAllister would see in bicycle riding henceforth the most modest and healthful of exercises of American girls, and he knows it. Wardie better come to Northville and see how gay and pretty our young ladies look on their wheels.[2]

The late nineteenth century saw a surge of physical feats—and feet—not seen in such number since the days of the Greek Olympics. A rage of walking and running races took hold of the nation, and spectators came for miles to watch as panting, sweating racers hauled their way to the finish line.

A foot race held in Northville in October 1876 was among those events, drawing many racing devotees to cheer—and wager—on the runners. Northville residents Purd Sessions, Sam Johnson, James Savage, Walter Bloy, and Charles Renwick, along with Cal Platt and Eugene Johnson of Plymouth, were the contenders in the strenuous match. Three heats were run in the course of the day, with Purd Sessions winning all three victoriously. Second place did not come quite so easily. The *Northville Record* reported, "As there was a tie between Sam Johnson and Bloy, they came to the score both determined to take third money, but with a good deal of exertion on the part of Bloy, he reached the rope about a foot ahead of Sam. Time 11 seconds." The race was an unequivocal success, bringing "a very large crowd of people from the surrounding towns, and was a fine race throughout."[3]

The American racing phenomenon began a few years earlier, specifically back to the fall of 1867. At that time, the country was experiencing a "walking mania," a craze that lasted throughout the autumn and winter. No fewer than seven separate long-distance walks were made by men in the Michigan area during the last week of November alone. Most likely, the instigator of all this long-distance walking was the famed pedestrian, Edward Payton Weston, age 28 in 1867. He had established himself some years earlier when he walked from Boston to Washington, D.C. to witness the inauguration of Abraham Lincoln. In 1867, he created a nationwide furor by claiming to be able to walk over 1,300 miles, from Portland, Maine, to Chicago, in 26 days.

Other "walkists" and "runnists" made names for themselves at the same time, spurred on, no doubt, by the far-reaching fame of Weston. In early November, a most novel race involving three Indians against three horses was held in Hamtramck. The horses ran a relay of 6 miles, while the Indians ran 3.25 miles. At the Hamtramck racecourse, the three Indians, Deerfoot, Steeprock, and Stevens, lined up with mares Lamplighter, Lady Ellis, and Victor Hugo. The $300 winning purse served to make things a bit more interesting. One of the Indians had quite a reputation on the running circuit. According to the *Detroit Advertiser and Tribune*, "The Indians are well-known throughout this country as very fleet and enduring, but of them, Deerfoot is by far the most famous, having been celebrated for his feats in this respect for over 10 years, both in this country and in England. As a 10-mile runner, he unquestionably has no superior in the world."[4]

Deerfoot, also known as Louis Bennet, was America's first great long-distance runner. In 1863, he established two new standards for the one-hour run, the last of which remained for over three decades. John Steeprock was also nationally known. He had come in second in the first distance race of any kind in the United States, held in 1844 in Hoboken, New Jersey.

Traditionally footraces were usually sponsored by horse-racing tracks and the Detroit race was no exception. Deerfoot started the relay, reeling off a 64 second quarter mile. The horses were not to be outdone. Lamplighter galloped to a 2:25 first mile, followed by Lady

The Northville–Wayne County Fair was a bustling and exciting place, as can be seen in this photograph. (NHS.)

Ellis in 2:45 and Victor Hugo in 2:35. The finish was close. "Upon the horses and men coming," reported the *Advertiser and Tribune*, "each party loudly claimed the race, but after careful investigation and deliberation, it was awarded to the Indians."[5]

From Jackson to Detroit, foot races continued to make the headlines, and throughout the statewide fervor, Edward Weston walked on. From October through December 1867, the *Detroit Daily Advertiser & Tribune* traced Weston's progress eagerly, following his travels each step of the way. The paper expressed every admiration for Weston and his 1,300-mile trek. It was reported that over 50,000 people lined the Chicago streets to witness the completion of Weston's walk of Thanksgiving Day, 1867. No less than a hero's welcome attended the nattily-dressed young man, and no detail, from his accompanying carriage to his complete costume, was overlooked in the report. Even a popular song, entitled "Weston's March to Chicago," was written to commemorate the sportsman's success.

From the race run by Purd Sessions and his friends in 1876, Northville has continued to attract runners. The Roadrunner Classic, which has been run through Northville since 1993, originated in Livonia nine years earlier. It, like the *Detroit Free Press* International Marathon, a 26.2-mile race that runs through two counties, attracts thousands of runners from all over. Though nineteenth-century sports fans may not have had the Boston Marathon to root for, there were still plenty of unique and unusual pedestrian feats to keep the public well entertained from coast to coast.

Another type of racing that has become synonymous with Northville is harness racing. It is an old tradition in this area. Long before Northville became the site of a permanent racetrack, the area was a popular one for such sport. As early as 1869, the *Wayne County Record* reported the following on an informal local race: "Mr. Chas. Houk and Mr. James Connolly matched their horses to run to Plymouth and back, 10 miles, both being harnessed. Connolly's horse came in ahead, having made the trip in 44 minutes. Stakes were put up but to no great amount."[6]

Some 24 years later, a race track in Plymouth drew crowds of up to 3,000 in one day to watch what were termed by the *Northville Record* as "the greatest and most successful races ever witnessed in the village of Plymouth." Competing in these contests, however, were not horses, but dogs. Even so, huge crowds showed up during each of the three-day competitions.

Popular as racing was in the late nineteenth century, it gained even more prominence in the 1900s. Even before the Northville Downs Racetrack became a reality during the World War II years, there had been other activities on the same site. At the turn of the century, the former swampland at Center Street and Seven Mile Road was first turned into a private nine-hole golf course by its owner, Ed Starkweather. Starkweather gradually changed the purpose of the area to create a modest racetrack for local contenders, with races every Sunday. In the absence of any grandstand, viewers gathered on picnic tables to watch their favorite steeds round the track.

By 1916, this homemade racecourse had evolved into the Northville–Wayne County Fair. It maintained its track and attracted horse lovers from all over the state. The fair was a success, lasting six days each year and drawing thousands of visitors from all over Michigan. By the 1930s, it was considered by the *Northville Record* to be one of the most outstanding fairs in Michigan, with one of the best half-mile tracks in the state.

111

Nighttime harness racing was a novelty when it started in Michigan at the Northville Downs Racetrack in 1944. Northville Downs, an outgrowth of the Northville–Wayne County Fair, has changed its look considerably over the years. Here, in 1965, it still had an open-air seating, unlike today's totally enclosed viewing area. (NHS.)

Racing was not the only use made by the Northville fairgrounds. In August 1939, boxer Joe Louis, "the Brown Bomber," used the grounds as a training site for his world championship match later that year. According to the *Northville Record*, "All floor work, punching, sparring and rope jumping will be done at the fairgrounds ring." Constructed especially for Louis, the boxing ring at the fairgrounds drew great crowds who witnessed his exhibition bouts in preparation for his Detroit fight in September against Bob Pastor.

During World War II, local fairs throughout the nation took a turn for the worse, and Northville's fair was no exception. However, by 1944, a group of businessmen from Buffalo, New York, approached the Northville Driving Club, which now owned the fairgrounds, with a novel idea. Nighttime harness racing at Northville Downs was proposed, much to the scorn of the Driving Club members, led by retired Northville physician Linwood Snow. But the Buffalo representatives were persistent, convinced their unusual idea would succeed.

On September 1, 1944, Michigan saw its first nighttime harness race at the Northville track. The venture surpassed even the most skeptical doubters, and harness racing has continued on the site, without interruption, ever since. With the success of the racetrack, the county fair was disbanded.

In 1956, the idea of a racetrack in Novi was considered. The community was, for the most part, in favor of the project, which was hoped to bring in thousands of dollars in revenue each year, as Northville's had been doing. The City of Northville reportedly received about $90,000 as its share of the receipts each year, and it was an inviting prospect for the neighboring town. One choice for the proposed site was along Meadowbrook Road between Eleven Mile and Grand River. However, the plan never made it to the starting gate, and Northville's former fairgrounds remains the only racetrack in the area.

The Northville fairgrounds was the site of a rodeo only one time in its history. In August 1943, at the 27th Northville Free Fair, there was steer wrestling, calf roping, and bronco and bull riding. "The midway and the arena were ablaze in the Northville Fairgrounds," reported the *Detroit News*. The rodeo, its main attraction for that year, was directed by Joe Greer and included among its performers the Horseback Quadrille from the Rambling Acres Farm at Plymouth.

According to an account written by Northville's eighth-grade classes in 1954, three accidents marred the program, all caused by the Brahma bull- and bronco-riding events. "All the people at the rodeo were frightened when the old ambulance came sputtering up," the children reported. "The Village of Northville did not have money to support [the rodeos], so we have had horse shows ever since then."[7]

Northville's many parks and numerous hills make it a mecca for other sporting events. Living in Northville, one is never far from a hill of some kind to be found for sports such as sledding and tobogganing, and the activity has been a popular one for years.

Tobogganing, which became popular in the late 1800s, began with rather practical uses. For example, in Michigan's Upper Peninsula, toboggans were used to transport passengers between Sault Ste. Marie and St. Ignace before the roads were built. Then, in 1881, the world's first tobogganing club was formed in Montreal, Canada. Two years later, the sport was launched with the first toboggan race in Switzerland, where winter resorts were becoming fashionable. New types of toboggans continued to be invented and the turn of the century saw the sport gain rapidly in popularity throughout the world.

Northville's Buchner Hill, the highest point in Wayne County, was the site of many a toboggan race down its steep slope in the late nineteenth and early twentieth centuries. Located near Allen Terrace Senior Citizen Home, above High Street and south of Hillside Middle School, Buchner Hill once stood majestically alone, with no houses below to impede the progress of a downhill toboggan run.

In 1885, landowner John Buchner had originally hoped to divide his land into a number of elegant, choice lots, all with magnificent views, that would lead up the hill towards his mansion at the top. His plan never materialized, however, as the homes built on the streets leading up to the hill never reached more than halfway up. Because the trees had already been cleared, though, for the homes that were never built, the spot became an ideal one for winter sports.

In the early 1900s, local children were able "to fly" as their sleds sped down the icy slope all the way to the fairgrounds, where Northville Downs now stands. According to a 1910 account in the *Northville Record*, "A full half mile ride can be had in just twenty seconds . . . Often as many as a hundred youngsters will be in the game at one time."[8] Though accidents resulting in broken limbs tended to slow the sport now and then, on the whole the hill was considered a comparatively safe venture considering the number of coasters that used it every year and the incredible rate of speed at which they traveled.

Winter was not the only time for sporting on Buchner Hill. In the late 1800s, the hill was the summertime site of many an action-filled bicycle competition, with many riders

Skiing was a popular winter pastime in hilly Northville. The ski tournament seen here was held in January 1924.

attempting to reach the pinnacle—most in vain. In later years, the hill became famous for "testing out city-made automobiles." The *Northville Record* reported the following in 1909:

> one of the big Detroit [automobile] companies kept one of their new model machines here in charge of experts for several weeks trying out its weak and strong points on hill climbing.
>
> Demonstrators with prospective customers often run out here from the city and mount the hill to show what the car will do. They all get to the top, but halfway is the limit for the "high speed" gear.[9]

Buchner Hill, now privately owned, is no longer the site of sledding or bicycle races. But Northville continues to carry on its tradition of downhill winter fun, from gentle frontyard inclines to the more exhilarating slopes of Hines Park toboggan runs.

Another winter sport in the area is curling. Curling has evolved from a little-known sport played in cold climates only to an Olympic event. It is an ancient game, played on the ice, that originated in Scotland in the sixteenth century. The game is played using heavy stones, which are hurled by hand along a smooth stretch of ice. A player delivers two stones, alternately with his opponent, from one end of the playing area to the target, about 42 yards away. The delivery of 16 stones by both teams completes the end. The team that places a stone closest to the target wins. Sweeping the ice with brooms helps create more friction, as well as a smoother surface, making it easier for the stone to slide.

Curling began in the United States right here in Michigan. The first club in the United States was the Orchard Lake Curling Club, organized around 1832. The members of this club used hickory blocks for "stones." A few years later, other clubs were formed in

Detroit and by 1885, they all merged to become the Detroit Curling Club, the oldest private club in Michigan. The club moved from its Detroit location near today's Wayne State University campus, to West Bloomfield in 1980. That building was recently sold, and before finding a permanent home, the Detroit Curling Club played "home" games in Windsor, Ontario.

While today's games are usually played in indoor ice arenas from November to March, the games played in Detroit in the nineteenth century were, by necessity, played on frozen rivers and depended solely on the weather. Curling, while a popular game, was slow to gain recognition. The *Detroit Free Press* in the late 1800s described it as "a capital game," but one "which the lovers of sports on the ice in this country have not yet learned to appreciate. It takes but a brief experience to make one an admirer of this rare fun."[10]

Though Detroiters participated in the sport with great enthusiasm, the sport was—and is—more a Canadian pastime than an American one. There are, however, a number of clubs in various states, particularly Wisconsin, North Dakota, and Minnesota, besides Michigan. Many Northville residents are members of the Detroit Curling Club, including its past president, Linda Handyside.

In 1879, it was reported that arrangements had been made for matches during the coming winter with curling clubs at London, Chatham, Sarnia, and Thamesville, Ontario; Toledo, Ohio; and Orchard Lake. Early curling matches were held on the frozen Detroit Athletic Club field at Woodward and Canfield before moving inside in 1906. It was originally a club for men, but women were allowed to become "Rockettes" in the 1950s. Eventually, family membership became accepted.

Like softball teams today, many companies organized curling matches. One such contest even reached the newspaper: "A curling match came off on Saturday," reported a

Henry Hall, Detroit's world champion skier, competed in this 1924 ski tournament on Northville's icy slopes.

The world champion Detroit Baseball Club is seen here in 1887, the year they joined the National League.

February 1862 issue of the *Detroit Free Press*, "between some Scotch gentlemen connected with the Detroit and Milwaukee and Great Western Railways, and some merchants of this city. The match was decided against the merchants."

Curling continues to be an exciting, fun-filled sport. As the *Free Press* exclaimed in 1862, "Should the weather continue favorable we shall expect to see the frozen surface of the river the field of more than one lively and exciting curling match."[11]

Summertime sports also reign in Northville. There is a good deal of controversy over the fact that Abner Doubleday of Cooperstown, New York, claimed to have invented the game of baseball in 1839, since the term "baseball" is believed to date as far back as the mid-eighteenth century. In addition, a game had existed for centuries in which a player hit an object with a stick and ran around one or more bases. It is most generally accepted that American baseball was directly derived from the British game of cricket, which was a form of an earlier game known as "rounders," or "roundball." An early version of baseball in America was known by boys as "old one cat" or "old two cat," depending on the number of bases used in the game.

By the mid-1800s, baseball had become an American sensation, and teams sprang up in towns throughout the country. Detroit was an early fan of the sport, organizing a team in 1865. Two years later, an unusual game took place in January. Apparently unwilling to wait until the spring thaw, the players wore skates and played on an ice rink. The novelty drew an understandably large crowd.

In August 1869, the Northville "Eclipse" baseball team played the Plymouth "Lone Stars" in Northville. After nine long innings, the Northville team finally won—by a score of 53 to 36. Such figures are incredible by today's standards, where a match of 1-0 is not uncommon. To get such a score, however, the game lasted almost four hours. Only one home run was scored during the entire game, hit by an Eclipse team member.

A number of baseball clubs were formed in the Detroit area during the 1870s. These amateur clubs eventually grew in stature, and professional baseball came to Detroit in 1881, with the team known as the "Detroits." By 1887, the Detroit Baseball Club had joined the National League, winning the world's championship that year against St. Louis. The "Detroits" became the "Detroit Tigers" in 1900 when the team joined the American League.

Meanwhile, amateur teams abounded. In July 1876, two teams from Northville's Michigan School Furniture Company played a rowdy match on the grounds of Charles Yerkes's farm, south of Base Line (Eight Mile) Road. The woodworkers formed one team, calling themselves the "Wood Butchers," while the moulders on the other side were known as the "Iron Mongers." Captains of the teams were W. John Little for the Wood

Northville's baseball team, seen here c. 1894, was a proud-looking club. Two of Northville's top players have been identified as Harry German (seated on the floor at right) and Thadd Knapp (back row, wearing the white tie). (NHS.)

117

Butchers and Milton J. Withee for the Iron Mongers. The game was wild and wooly, as balls flew in all directions and "the fun ran high." Players, however, tended to forget they were playing hardball, apparently thinking they were playing the child's game of "old two cat," and several injuries added to the excitement of the day. The *Northville Record* covered the game with a watchful eye: "One gentleman of Little's side was the recipient of . . . the ball full in the eye, compelling his immediate retirement from the field. Another was hit square on the ear and that organ assumed a size not usual in ordinary beings. By good luck no one was killed outright . . ." The game came to its agonizing end, with the Wood Butchers as victors, winning by a score of 28 to 24.[12]

By 1885, Northville had a team called the Northville Town Team. It existed for about five years. Around 1910, another organization known as the Circle N (for Northville) was created. According to *A History of Northville*, the Circle N had statewide renown because it beat many Detroit teams—a major challenge even then—and produced some fine local players as well. The Detroit House of Corrections sponsored a baseball team, known as the "Dehocoites." The Plymouth team's exploits were followed diligently by the *Northville Record*. One game, played in Lansing against the Sunoco Keystones in the summer of 1929, ended in a score of 8 to 7, in favor of the "Dehocoites." The *Record* reported, "It took 11 innings to settle this encounter, but Dehoco finally emerged victorious . . ."[13]

Baseball continues to be America's favorite sport, with Little League and softball among the most popular pastimes. From its first days on vacant lots to today's specially designed stadiums, participants and viewers alike still get that special tingle when they hear those inspiring words: "Play ball!"

Football came to the United States in 1869, when Rutgers University competed with Princeton players in what was the first American college football game ever. Based on the British game of rugby, it resembled a soccer game more than football as we know it today, with rules that excluded throwing or running with the ball. The ball, unlike the traditional oval pigskin used today, was much rounder in the nineteenth century. From a team of 25 players on each side in 1869, the number of players has since been cut to 11 per team.

Football seeped into America's heritage. Northville was the proud home of a number of football teams over the years, most notably from Northville High School. Their exploits received considerable newspaper coverage, even from their earliest years, and it seemed that, to the *Northville Record*, they could do no wrong. In December 1898, the *Record* wrote of its favorite sons. They quoted a disparaging remark from the *Plymouth Mail* that dared to shine an unpleasant light on the home team. "When it comes to foot-ball," the Plymouth paper scorned, "Northville isn't in it." The *Record* was quick to defend such blasphemy by refuting, "Northville is hardly one-third licked yet . . ."[14] The paper praised the town's boys by calling them gentlemen in the face of adversity, and losing 22-0 to the Plymouth team was barely anything to be concerned with.

The sport continued to gain popularity nationwide, and by 1908, when Jim Thorpe became the star of the Carlisle Indians football team, his name was a household word. In 1921, the Professional National Football League was organized, and the first Superbowl was played in 1964. In all the subsequent years of national football frolics, however, none could quite match the excitement and drama of a game played in November 1929, between those old rivals, Northville and Plymouth High Schools. The game was covered

Located about 20 miles west of Detroit, the Northville-Plymouth area was a day's outing in the 1920s. Tourists could even camp overnight in the park now known as Hines Park.

in much detail by the adoring *Northville Record*, and the pride in their local team—which had improved considerably since the previous century's tournaments—shines through in the following:

> Northville's high school football team won its yearly clash with the strong Plymouth high team Saturday in a game featured by hard football and good playing on the part of both contesting teams. The victory, a 7 to 0 contest, was a hard earned one and showed how closely the two teams were matched.
>
> The field was a sea of mud and both teams were somewhat handicapped because of this condition. The water soaked ball made passing practically impossible and the kickers of the teams made but little yardage through their efforts.
>
> The orange and black's first chance to score came when Huff caught the kickoff and ran 65 yards to the Plymouth 20 yard line before being downed . . . Northville's defense was strong, in fact the whole team played a remarkable good game . . .[15]

One site for ballgames in the Northville area for many years has been Hines Park. The Wayne County Park System began in 1919. In the 1920s, the Wayne County Road Commission began to acquire land that would be used for a park patterned after the Bronx Parkway in New York. Edward Hines Drive, named for the first Wayne County road commissioner, meanders more than 17 miles following the course of the Rouge River between Dearborn and Northville. The drive cuts through Edward Hines Park, which is actually composed of several small roadside parks and other parcels of land that were combined to comprise one large county park.

The Simons siblings with their cousin Sam enjoyed visits to Hines Park. This shot was taken in the fall of 1938 in the Cass Benton Woods area of the park. (Popkin.)

The first piece of land used for this purpose was land willed to the County by Northville resident Cass Benton. Benton was an early member of the Wayne County Road Commission. When he died, he willed his farm to Wayne County for use as a park after his wife passed away. However, in 1925, Mrs. Benton gave her property to the County so that she would be able to see her husband's wish come true. Historian Mina Humphries Varnum's description of the idyllic scene in 1927 still applies today:

> If you wish to see what has been made of [Benton's] old sugaring grove, drive
> out Seven Mile Road nearly to Northville and turn to your left . . . A short run
> of about a mile will bring you to the entrance of Cass Benton Park, one of the
> most beautiful park sites in the county, comprising 16 acres of wooded land.[16]

The picturesque red-brick "comfort stations" that still dot the park were built during the 1920s. Though new, modern facilities have begun to replace the crumbling relics of the past, the memory of their unique architecture is still evident in the twenty-first century. The "Shelter-Comfort Station," which was located in Cass Benton Park was built in 1927. At that time, it was open day and night, with attendants on duty at all times. Drinking fountains throughout the park were connected with Plymouth's water supply.

Across the road from the Cass Benton Park sits a sign which reads, "Bennett Arboretum." "Jessie Merrill Bennett started the first public arboretum in the state of Michigan," explained Nancy Darga, chief of design for the Wayne County Park System, and author of a book about Hines Park. There was what Darga calls a "hopscotch plan" of acquiring pieces of land for the park. "Henry Ford was the biggest helper," she said, in developing the park. By building his village industries all along the proposed parkway, he would donate land to the Wayne County Road Commission to be used as part of the park system.[17]

The latest pieces of land to be added to the park did not come about until the 1960s, with additions in Dearborn. Darga explained that, in the year 2000, there was still one last piece to connect the entire parkway, at Newburgh and Hines Drive in Livonia. Those who live near what is now Hines Park are truly fortunate to be so close to such natural beauty. Commenting on the park's atmosphere, Varnum wrote the following at the beginning of the twentieth century:

> Quite probably your first emotion will be a feeling of relief that the hand of improvement has not robbed the grove of its natural charm and beauty; but that the original rolling contour of the land has been preserved and the irregularly placed trees . . . have been left as they were . . .

Summer in Northville is indeed a lively time. Northville's Fourth of July parades are so popular that one day in 1987, a television crew came to town and staged a mock parade for nationwide commercial viewing. July 4, 1776, of course, started it all. While Detroit was celebrating its 75th year of existence, the 13 eastern colonies declared themselves independent from England. The first celebration of this historic event came one year later. In 1777, Congress also adopted the flag featuring the stars and stripes that still represent the United States.

City dwellers were able to enjoy leisurely summer days in Hines Park. This view was taken around 1928.

Detroit, still under British rule, however, did not participate in the festivities. On July 11, 1796, the British finally evacuated the city and turned it over to the United States. One year later, the new American city of Detroit was finally able to celebrate its first Independence Day along with the rest of the country. Freedom continued in Detroit until the War of 1812, when, in August of that year, the city was once again surrendered to the encroaching British. It remained under the British flag for one year. The city has celebrated its independence from foreign rule ever since.

One July 4 occurrence in 1871 included the dedication of the new Detroit City Hall. The Centennial celebration was widespread throughout the country. Detroiters enjoyed a processional, street decorations, boat races, fireworks, and more. In Northville, "the centennial Fourth of July was observed in our village in a very satisfactory manner," declared the *Northville Record* of July 14, 1876, "although the program which had been advertised could not be carried out by reason of a severe storm, which continued until afternoon." As soon as the storm abated, "the people began to come into town so that by 2 p.m. several hundred had collected." The festivities included a 13-gun salute at midnight, "and a general din of lesser noise was kept up through the day." A parade also marked the event.

As the years went by, the day began to get less political and more recreational. "A large crowd witness[ed] the sports" on July 4, 1893, in Plymouth. The *Northville Record* reported on a number of sporting events that took place that day, including a ball game against the Northville team—Plymouth won, 15 to 11. Races of all forms took over the rest of the day, including horse races, a footrace, and even a bicycle race, where Northville's Thad Knapp was the fourth-place winner. The patriotic flavor of the day, however, seemed to be missing. The *Record* commented that "the decorations were very scant and one had to hunt a long time to find a flying flag . . . there were a few, a very few, one cent flags scattered here and there about the village."[18]

Patriotism was to return with world unrest in the twentieth century. Large public-spirited ads in the *Northville Record* throughout the 1940s promoted patriotism, freedom, and safety. "Be alive on the 5th" was a common phrase. A day of sports, games, picnics, and races was still the order of the day during those war-torn years. The annual parade, however, did not make a regular appearance until 1947, with a "pet and costume parade" for youngsters. By the next year, the Northville High School band led the processional and the tradition that still continues was on its way.

Clowns, wild animals, acrobats, and death-defying stunts all add up to the greatest show on earth, and the excitement and thrills of today's circus. Though most of the circuses seen today seat thousands in arenas such as Detroit's Joe Louis Arena or the Pontiac Silverdome, the majority of circuses in America before the 1950s were performed under large canvas tents.

Picture the elephants, lumbering slowly but steadily, as they help unfurl the massive tents. The smell of sawdust hangs in the air, and all the circus personnel take on multiple roles, from setting up chairs to juggling under the spotlight, from selling popcorn to taming wild animals. This may sound like a scene from the past, but Northville and nearby Novi have both been the sites of the traditional, old-fashioned tent shows in recent years.

Tent shows are not a thing of the past in small communities like Novi, Northville, and Plymouth. Though this photo of a tent show elephant and handler in Detroit dates to the early part of the twentieth century, a similar view can still be seen today when the circus comes to town.

The Franzen Brothers Circus played at Novi's Lakeshore Park in August 1986. One year later, Northville saw the big top rise at Northville Downs Racetrack, converting an ordinary parking lot into a place of magic and delight. The Great American Circus, like others of times past, made use of their hardworking elephants to erect and dismantle the tent, as well as for performing elaborate routines during the show.

The circus is an ancient form of entertainment, and has been bringing pleasure to audiences for centuries. When brought to America from Europe in the late eighteenth century, the circus took on a completely new look. Few cities in the new country were financially able to support the permanent circus theaters still seen in European cities today, and a new form was needed. The portable tent show, setting up fairly quickly and moving completely from town to town, proved to be an instant success, and by the 1820s, the big top was an American institution.

While European circuses still perform in one ring, the multi-ring show is unique to America. The second ring was introduced in the 1870s, and a prime showman named P.T. Barnum and his partner James Bailey created the three-ring circus ten years later. The circus was a popular form of amusement for nineteenth-century Detroit-area residents. Bailey's Circus performed in Detroit in 1864. Along with equestrian and acrobatic feats, the circus presented a clown named Jimmy Reynolds as the featured performer.

In 1869, a tent show in Plymouth had near-disastrous results when a rainstorm collapsed the huge tent. Though the scene that followed was described as "laughable" by the *Wayne County Record*, the paper admitted that "had there been a large crowd, severe accidents might have been the result."[19]

P.T. Barnum was a show in himself. In 1877, the *Northville Record* exclaimed gleefully of the impending visit in July of the venerable showman to Detroit and Ann Arbor. The paper raved, "There is only one Barnum and the veteran is coming . . . Barnum a greater curiosity than all the wonderful objects with which his present 'Greatest Show on earth' abounds." Barnum's appearance at each show was guaranteed, and readers were enthusiastically encouraged to attend.[20]

Ringling Brothers, the current successor to Barnum, performed their last tent show in 1956, and the number of traveling troupes soon dropped significantly throughout the country. The few circus companies that have come to the Northville area are in the minority. Today, only a handful of traveling shows still exist, performing to small-town crowds. Despite television, men in space, computers, and modern technology, the old-fashioned tent shows are still able to enthrall and mesmerize, as they have for hundreds of years.

The history of theater in the Detroit area dates back to the early nineteenth century. Though Detroit was founded in 1701, it was not until the town became a city under the military command of General Alexander Macomb that art gained focus in the area. Military troops stationed in Detroit after the War of 1812 began to put on plays, with the men playing all the roles. Soldiers' wives did help out, but only behind the scenes by painting scenery and sewing costumes. A decade later, the first amateur theatrical organization was created in the form of the Thespian Society in 1826.

As Detroit grew, the quality of life continued to improve with more churches, schools, businesses, and organizations developing daily. The cultural arts were not left behind. The first touring dramatic company came to Detroit during the summer of 1827. Performances were held in a brick barn owned by Ben Woodwarth. Other touring companies began to visit Detroit and continued to perform at Woodwarth's barn.

Detroit's City Theater opened in 1834, the first permanent theater in the city, which drew prominent actors to its stage. Professional as well as amateur productions continued to flourish in the Detroit area over the years.

The lights dim, the orchestra tunes up, and the curtain opens to a scene of fantasy and enchantment. In the days before movies and television, live theater was the main escape from the everyday, routine life of most people. Theater in America, as in Europe, thrived because of the desire for entertainment and relaxation for the early pioneers. "Theater," however, had always carried a somewhat negative connotation and the term "opera house," first used in this country in reference to a Philadelphia theater in the late 1700s, was considered somehow more refined.

After the Civil War, opera houses began to be built in most of the country's larger cities, including Detroit. The Detroit Opera House gave its first symphony concert in November 1869. Some of the greatest dramatic actors of the day performed there, including Edwin Booth and Minnie Maddern, later known as Mrs. Fiske. Her father, Tom Davey, was manager of the Detroit Opera House for a number of years in the late 1800s. The Detroit Opera House, which faced downtown Detroit's Campus Martius, also contained J.L. Hudson's clothing store on the first floor.

Northville was not immune to culture, but the story of Northville's Opera House had a hard and painful beginning. The idea of an opera house in Northville was conceived by

The Detroit Opera House, seen in the background at right, first opened in 1869. Another symbol of entertainment in Detroit can be seen in the foreground: Sanders Pavilion, which served ice cream and other delicacies beginning in the 1890s.

Northville Record publisher Samuel Little. What began as a simple push for culture grew to become an obsession that followed Little until his final days in the town. In fact, the project eventually took so much of his time that often the newspaper suffered, getting out late because of Little's other pressing commitments.

In late 1876, the plans for the opera house were developed and fund-raisings began early the next year. The first "grand concert in aid of the Northville Opera House" was held in January 1877 at the Young Men's Hall. Following what was billed as "the finest concert ever given in Northville," the *Northville Record* reported with satisfaction on the success of the venture.

Little's urging to newspaper readers to contribute to this worthwhile cultural effort was evident in his front-page articles reporting on each aspect of the building's progress. But it proved a long, slow, agonizing process. Though Northville residents may have wanted to add to the cultural refinement of their town, it took much time and money for it to finally materialize. Located at the southeast corner of Dunlap and Center Streets, the foundation of the building was completed in November 1877, but the doors didn't open for another two years for its first performance. It is unknown whether Little was even around to see his dream come into reality, as he was last heard of in the Northville area in December 1879.

The opera house existed for many years, however, and by 1892 was known as the Moffat Opera House, with a seating capacity of 800. Stores occupied the first floor and part of the building was used for offices of the *Northville Record*. The *Detroit Free Press* called the building "the masterpiece of a German artist." Musical concerts were not the only venue to perform at the theater. "Among the less glamorous ventures which held sway in the house at one time," wrote the *Detroit Free Press* in 1949, "was a Kickapoo Indian Medicine Show."[21]

In 1950, the owner of the building had it razed to the ground rather than sell it to Henry Ford for restoration in Greenfield Village. At the time of its demise, the Northville Opera House was reportedly the oldest one standing in Michigan. Culture has not died in Northville, but the era of the majestic opera house in America is long gone.

Another American custom that has come and gone is an institution known in the late nineteenth and early twentieth centuries as the "Chautauqua." The name is unfamiliar to most generations today, but long before the television era, it was a frequent diversion combining education with entertainment in the form of concerts, plays, and lectures, often held in an outdoor tent.

The name comes from Chautauqua, New York, a small town in the southwestern part of the state. It is located on Chautauqua Lake, where a summer adult education program started in 1874. The annual summer educational and recreational assembly began in New York, but spread throughout the United States. By the 1900s, President Theodore Roosevelt was quoted as calling the Chautauqua "the most American thing in America."[22]

In Northville, the Chautauqua was a well-anticipated annual event. It started in the town in 1913. During the years of the first World War, patriotism ran high, and the Northville Chautauqua of 1917 was especially meaningful. The *Northville Record* promoted the event well over a month in advance, promising the 1917 Chautauqua to be a "big success" and a "Patriotic year in the Chautauqua," with a special "Patriotic Day" held during the festivities. "The spirit of patriotism will ring in with music on each of the five days," the *Record* vowed.

The program ran from July 27 to August 1, 1917. The week-long event concluded with a pageant entitled *A Night at the Fairy Carnival*, in which the 75 characters in the play would be portrayed by the children themselves. The only requirement was a 75¢ season ticket, which included a special costume for each young actor. "To all boys and girls who earn their own money to buy the season ticket," noted the *Record*, "will be given an honor badge of special distinction."

Other first-time special features of the 1917 event included "a company of negro jubilee singers, under the leadership of W.A. Hann, giving soulful tunes of the old plantations and the wonderfully soothing melodies of the southland." "Band Day" was another "thrilling" event. "Our band this year is the best we have ever had on the Chautauqua," boasted the *Record*, "led by Francesco Pallaria, who is dynamic, dramatic and decidedly spectacular." It was surely an occasion no one would dare to miss. A Handel Choir was the finale of the week, consisting of both "masterpieces of sacred music . . . and popular gems from light and grand opera."

After the whirlwind week, the results were in: "1917 Chautauqua Gratifying Success," proclaimed the *Record*. Northville's fourth Chautauqua was praised, overall, as the "best ever." Though there were some disappointments, the *Northville Record* dismissed these by claiming that the uncommonly high quality of the first program given by the Mrs. Wilbur Starr Concert Party made everything else pall in its shadow. Despite any misgivings, however, the event concluded without a deficit—much to the relief of the Chautauqua planners—and a good feeling throughout the community. "This season's event," the *Record* claimed, "has left Northville people more firmly convinced than ever that our town cannot afford to do without the Chautauqua as an annual event."[23] Alas, as with other customs, the Chautauqua has been replaced—by motion pictures, television, and videos— consigned to remain a thing of the past.

Back at the turn of the nineteenth century, band concerts were at their peak of popularity. Town bands, consisting mainly of wind and percussion instruments, began some 400 years ago in Europe. They were originally created to announce the hours from town hall towers, but they gradually went on to perform as part of church services. Eventually, they found their way outside to entertain at civic events, and the idea of a town band has been around ever since. By the 1700s, band concerts were mostly light classical pieces still heard today, by such composers as Haydn and Mozart.

Marching bands gained prominence under Napoleon and soon caught on in the young United States. The U.S. Marine Corps Band, formed in 1798, is the oldest American band still in existence. The music of the marching band, used in the military for parades and at football games today, was found to inspire and encourage the participants in the various events.

The town band gained its greatest fame in the United States when John Philip Sousa led the Marine Corps Band. After working with them for 12 rousing years, Sousa formed his own concert band, and his travels throughout the country and the world made him a musical legend. Bands were formed in almost every town, and Northville was no exception.

The Northville Band was created in 1871 with the musicians led by James S. Savage. Six years later, the band was aiding in fund-raising events for the new opera house. In

Every town had its brass band, and Northville was no exception. Over the years, many groups were organized to provide musical entertainment. Here, the Northville Community School Band poses proudly for a portrait. (NHS.)

127

January 1877, the band, now under the direction of Professor J.H. Simonds, was deemed "a grand success" by the *Northville Record* for its presentation at a benefit for the opera house. The *Record* raved as follows:

> Prof. Simonds deserves no little credit for the splendid programme [*sic*] which was presented under his direction, and together with his extraordinary ability as a pianist and accompaniest [*sic*], won golden opinions from the large audience in attendance. This gentleman was formerly a resident of Northville, and his old and new friends received him very flatteringly, and he has good reason to feel proud of his success . . .[24]

A month later, the band's performance at the Young Men's Hall received similar accolades:

> The entertainment given by the Northville Band, Tuesday evening last was a most decided success. The house was well filled, and the proceeds will net quite a nice sum. The band shows a marked improvement under the tuition of the talented musician, Prof. J. Henry Gardner, the well-known and popular leader of the Flint City Band, who has had them in training the past week. Each selection was rendered with a correctness and precision that "astonished the natives," and reflected much credit on themselves and the Professor. The audience was highly pleased with the commendable and successful efforts of the band, and received them in good style.
>   Prof. Gardner appeared in full dress and executed several really fine cornet solos, which for the time, melody and effect were simply immense . . . This gentleman's efforts were enthusiastically acknowledged . . . The members of the band have every reason to feel proud of their Success, and also of their leader . . .[25]

The band did not limit their performances to local shows only. On July 4, 1878, they played in Saginaw and the *Saginaw Republican* labeled them as "one of the finest organizations of its size in the state."[26] The praise did not go to their heads, and the band continued to please audiences for years to come.

Northville residents were able to enjoy their favorite town's band at a highly visible vantage point. Nicknamed the "Crow's Nest," Northville's bandstand was a high-rise affair that stood at the intersection of Main and Center Streets for many years. The bandstand was torn down in the 1920s. Northville no longer has a crow's nest, but it does still have a bandstand downtown, where, on a summer's evening, music fills the air and one is—temporarily, at least—transported back to a time of straw hats and high-button shoes, and the lilting strains of a town band.

The late 1890s created a phenomenon that would change the world as much, if not more, than the automobile. In 1896, Thomas Edison's invention of a "vitascope" was exhibited to newspapermen at the Detroit Opera House. Another invention called the "biograph" made its debut the same year at Detroit's Wonderland Theater, and one year later something called the "phantograph" produced a smaller image but without what the

For many years, the Northville Band entertained passersby in the bandstand, or "crow's nest," downtown. It was located at the intersection of Center and Main Streets.

Detroit Free Press called "the usual blur." They all added up to become the first motion pictures, and their impact on the public would have a tremendous effect all over the world. The *Detroit Free Press* predicted in May 1896 that moving pictures were "bound to be popular." That would prove to be quite an understatement.

The first movie to be shown in Detroit was held at the Opera House in the summer of 1896. The short film depicted a bullfight in Mexico and was a memorable experience to all who witnessed it. As the years went by, the quality of motion or moving pictures improved slowly; the first theater to be devoted exclusively for movies in Detroit was the Casino Theatre, opened in 1905. Owned by John H. Kunsky and A. Arthur Caille, it was located on Monroe Avenue. By 1906, the first process for motion picture color photography, known as "kinecolor," was developed by G.A. Smith and Charles Urban, but it would be some time before the innovation caught on. However, the prediction made by the *Detroit Free Press* in 1896 came to pass, and by 1915 there were 17,000 movie theaters in the United States.

Northville's first movie theater was called the Alseum. It was destroyed by fire but was replaced in 1925 by the Penniman-Allen Theatre. Located at 133 Main Street, it showed movies for nearly a quarter of a century. The world's first all-talking picture, *The Lights of New York*, made its debut in 1928, and by 1929 Northville's Penn-Allen Theatre was ready to join the world of the "talkies." The *Northville Record* was ecstatic:

> Northville is going to have talking pictures—the best that can be secured, according to announcement just made by Harry Lush, manager of the Penniman-Allen Theatre.

129

Pending the installation of the new equipment, the theater will be closed for one week, beginning Monday, September 16 . . .

The theater owners will install the R.C.A. Photo-phone equipment, the best that is on the market for talking motion pictures.

Few communities the size of Northville anywhere in the country have talking pictures and the announcement will be greeted in Northville and vicinity with general approval from the many patrons of the Penniman-Allen Theatre.

Not only has it been the policy of the management to give the community the best there is in pictures, but it now takes the lead in providing Northville with high grade talking pictures.[27]

In October, the talking screen's first musical comedy, *The Cocoanuts*, was shown in Northville for a two-day run. The Penniman-Allen Theatre closed in 1953 because of what a 1954 Northville student publication called "a lack of interest." That interest would transfer itself to other forms of entertainment.

The 1920s brought about the growth of radio broadcasting, and Detroit was a pioneer in its history. The world's first radio station was Detroit's own WWJ. In February 1922, the Detroit Symphony Orchestra, led by Ossip Gabrilowitch, conductor, performed the first complete symphony concert in the country over the radio. It was broadcast by the "Detroit News" station, which would later be called WWJ.

WWJ was a leader in many radio firsts. In October 1924, Ty Tyson detailed the play-by-play action of a University of Michigan football game, the first ever done on radio. He repeated this pioneering effort with a similar description of the Detroit Tigers' opening

Formerly the Penniman–Allen Theatre, today's Marquis offers live children's theater, often featuring local youngsters in the performance. (Popkin.)

Though there are no movie theaters in Northville, theater is alive and well in the city. Children's theater is presented at the Marquis Theatre, while Genitti's Little Theatre , across the street, specializes in dinner theater productions. (Popkin.)

season baseball game at Detroit's Navin Field in September 1927, broadcast live from the field over WWJ radio. According to *A History of Northville*, the first radio in Northville was set up in the Methodist church by Clifford B. Turnbull in 1921, shortly after WWJ received the first radio license.

By 1947, a new form of communication was developed and eventually became an American pastime. "Though less than 100 families in the area had receivers, the state's first television station, WWJ-TV (Detroit), began daily broadcasts, consisting, at first, of test patterns and studio presentations."[28] Television came to Northville shortly after this first broadcast, and it was just a few years later that the Penniman-Allen Theatre would see its demise.

Television, as we all know, was not the flash-in-the-pan some skeptics claimed it would be. The first color television was seen in Michigan in 1951, the same year the first international TV broadcast would be held, once more with Detroit's WWJ-TV as the pioneering station.

Northville's movie theater made a brief comeback for a few years. It changed its name to the Marquis, but in the 1980s it also changed its format to feature live children's theater. The motion picture business has clearly not diminished over the years, but one still needs to go outside of Northville's boundaries to find a movie theater these days.

The latest entertainment trend is actually a throwback to the Beatnik era. Coffee houses have made a comeback, and several thrive in downtown Northville. These newest additions merely add to the multitude of diversions that make up Northville's recreational atmosphere.

10. TRAVEL

"You can't get there from here" was probably heard a lot in the eighteenth and early nineteenth centuries, especially in western territories like Michigan. Almost all early travelers to lower Michigan started out in Detroit, where, for nearly a century after its first settlement in 1701, travelers would remain. Very few dared to journey far from its comparative conveniences and security for a simple reason: once they landed in the port of Detroit, there really was no place to go. There were no roads leading out of Detroit, making it extremely difficult to settle lands within the interior of the state. Only Indian trails were available for traversing through the thick forests. Incredibly, many of these original trails have endured to become the roads we know today. Before these roads became the smooth concrete or asphalt strips we are familiar with, they began as crude muddy pathways among the trees.

Since lumber was so plentiful in Michigan, roads paved with wood were very popular. Plank roads increased in use by the passage of the Plank Road Act of 1848. Three-inch-thick planks, usually of oak, were laid across the roadbed. Though they formed a rough, uneven surface, they were considered superior to the dirt trails left by the Indians. Warping and rotting of the wood was a constant problem.

To support the maintenance of these roads, toll gates were set up at various intervals along each road. One of the first plank roads in the state—and the last to remain in existence—was the Grand River, or Detroit-Howell, Plank Road, which had grown from a well-worn Indian trail. By 1850, this road became a toll road, operated by the Detroit and Howell Plank Road Company. When the capital of Michigan was moved from Detroit to Lansing, construction began in full force for a good road connecting the two major cities. The Detroit-Howell Road was the most logical route and became planked in 1850.

Many of these old trails are still identifiable by the retention of an early name—Ann Arbor Trail and Pontiac Trail are two examples. Others have been more disguised. Michigan Avenue was known by the Indians as the Great Sauk Trail, running across the state from Detroit to Lake Michigan.

Plank roads were common in Michigan in the nineteenth century. This is a view of a Detroit street in the 1890s.

Once Detroit visitors of the 1800s were able to venture out of the city, other areas of the state were finally able to be explored, such as the Northville/Novi area in the mid-1820s. The road running between Novi and Walled Lake (now Novi Road) was planked in the 1850s. This improved travel conditions for farmers transporting their goods to Detroit and other markets. It took about three days for a Novi farmer to go to Detroit and back to sell his goods.

The American highway system suffered when the railroads came into widespread use beginning in the 1830s. Though improvements continued to be made to the roads, they were given second priority to the faster, more efficient railroads. Only after the turn of the century, with the advent of the automobile, did city planners realize the importance of maintaining good roads and highways.

In 1909, the country saw the first mile of concrete road laid out in Detroit on Woodward Avenue between Six and Seven Mile Roads. That year also saw the last of the plank toll roads, with the franchises for all the privately-owned toll gates expiring in April. The year 1929 saw the concrete paving of both Seven and Eight Mile Roads. Seven Mile was paved from Northville's limits, east to Farmington Road. By April, more men were hired for the work detail in order to get the 6-mile stretch completed by July. By paving Seven Mile with concrete, Northville became the first community in western Wayne County to be directly connected to Detroit with what was referred to as a "super-highway." Though Eight Mile was a state road, the responsibility for its being paved fell to the Wayne County Road Commission. By the mid-twentieth century, road construction in Michigan was a major concern.

133

This scene from Dearborn's Greenfield Village captures the essence of the stagecoach era.

The first regular transportation service in cities began in Paris in 1819 with a line of horse-drawn stagecoaches. Ten years later, a similar line, known as omnibuses, began running in London. America's first urban transportation began in New York in 1827, when Abraham Brower initiated a regular stagecoach service that traveled along Broadway. The service proved popular, and more routes were soon added. The stagecoach was America's first practical method of public transportation. Stagecoach travel was dirty, jarring, slow, and expensive, but there were few alternatives in the eighteenth and early nineteenth centuries. Bad roads aggravated the already uncomfortable ride. As roads improved gradually through the years, the demand for more stagecoach lines increased throughout the country.

In Michigan, the stagecoach was an important feature in providing travel and communication across the state. The earliest stagecoach line from Detroit to Howell was established in 1838. Running along the rutted, muddy Indian trail known then as the Detroit-Howell Road, the line was a well-used one and served Northville and Novi residents daily. However, it soon grew into terrible disrepair between Farmington and Novi, and wagons found it more convenient to take Eight or Nine Mile Road rather than get stuck in the mud and swamps of Grand River. The road suffered from poor conditions as late as 1913. Unfortunately, the stagecoach routes were set, and despite the unpleasant conditions, they had to travel along poorly maintained Grand River Road.

Two stages ran daily each way between Detroit and Howell, providing transportation for up to 24 passengers and freight at a time. Besides the Grand River Road line, there were many other stagecoach lines in the area. The Northville, Plymouth & Wayne Stage Line ran daily from Plymouth to Wayne, extending its service into Northville in 1869.

The safety of the stagecoach was an ever-present concern to passengers as well as stage owners. Some drivers were not quite as careful as they might have been. In June 1849, the *Detroit Free Press* described an accident that today would be listed in the newspaper's "Police Blotter" with an OUIL (operating under the influence of liquor) heading: "The driver of the Mt. Clemens stage was severely injured in front of the Railroad Hotel. In turning his stage around he fell from the seat and the wheels passed over his head and abdomen. His ear was cut off. It is said he was intoxicated."[1]

Jim Millar, the driver of the Northville stage line, on the other hand, was said to be "considered an adept in the art of driving, and attention to the comfort of his passengers, will," said the *Wayne County Record* with certainty, "make himself none the less popular on this end of the route."[2]

Today, the names of Hilton, Sheraton, and Ramada instill instant relief to any road-weary traveler coming to the end of his/her trail. Back in the early nineteenth century, there were no such respites for travelers who undoubtedly struggled through much harsher travel conditions than any airport- or freeway-fighter could ever imagine. By the time the territory of Michigan was created in 1805, with Detroit as its capital, settlers began their slow but steady stream into the new land. Since most of these newcomers arrived from New York State and other points east, Detroit soon became a bustling port of entry to the new territory. Then, when the Erie Canal opened in 1825, Michigan experienced a meteoric rise in its population. By 1836, as many as 2,000 immigrants were arriving in Detroit in a single day. During May alone, 90 steamboats stopped at Detroit wharves.

Once passengers arrived at the port of Detroit, western-bound travelers would head off along the old Chicago Road (of which Michigan Avenue is the present-day equivalent), where travel of 10 miles per day was considered good. After this grueling distance, settlers would come upon the place where the road met the Rouge River. At this propitious spot was the farm of Conrad "Coon" Ten Eyck, a prominent Detroiter from as early as 1815, who came originally from Albany, New York. The Ten Eyck farm in Dearborn covered several thousand acres. His tavern was a haven for travel-weary settlers and their families for over 50 years. In fact, most settlers traveling out of Detroit would spend their first night in the Michigan Territory at the Ten Eyck Tavern. At least one farm was turned into an inn for weary travelers, and that of Conrad "Coon" Ten Eyck was probably the most famous.

Legend has it, in fact, that the very nickname of Michigan state came from an encounter with "Coon" Ten Eyck. According to one account, "Many have heard of [Ten Eyck] treating a party from Detroit . . . to a wolf steak for dinner." Amazed at what they had eaten, one guest replied, " 'If we have eaten wolf, we must be wolverines.' Hence the name wolverines applied to settlers in this state."[3] Whatever the reason, Michigan is still known as the "Wolverine State."

From this point, the logical route for northwestern-bound pioneers was to follow close along the banks of the north branch of the Rouge River. This route roughly parallels the area between Evergreen or Lahser and Telegraph Roads today, which met up with Grand

River Road in Redford Township. Here, travelers continuing straight north would soon find themselves in Southfield or Bloomfield Township; those veering west on Grand River Road would pass through Farmington and Novi, where many of these pioneers began to settle.

In later years, as travelers would trod the muddy path known as Grand River Road, they would come upon another welcome hostelry in Farmington. The Botsford Inn was built in 1836 by Steven Jennings, designed as a hostel for sheep and cattle drivers going to Detroit. It also turned out to be a good stopping place for new settlers heading west out of Detroit, and the little inn grew in popularity. Purchased by the Botsford family in 1850, it was kept in the family until 1924, when it was sold to Henry Ford. He used it for many years as the site of his favored square dances, before selling the inn to a hotel chain in 1951.

Among the hotels in existence in the mid-nineteenth century was the Northville Hotel. Located on the northwest corner of Main and Hutton Streets, where Heritage Federal Savings now stands, it had been owned since 1835 by Michael Thompson. His brothers William and Phineas later took over the running of the hotel. Northville pioneer David Clarkson wrote in his memoirs that "Phineas was a very popular landlord, social, genial, good-hearted, charitable, friendly, and liked by all. Every pioneer will remember him as 'Phim. Thompson.' "[4] The hotel was purchased by Charles Houk in 1869.

Another hotel of this era was the Ambler House. This hotel was the headquarters for the stage routes leading to Detroit. According to an early account in the *Northville Record*, "This was the only means of communication then existing." The Ambler House was built in 1858 by William Ambler. Located on the southeast corner of Main and Center Streets, the Ambler House became a popular stagecoach stop. The *Record* explained, "In the early days Mrs. Ambler was well known throughout the country as the popular landlady of the

This view of a Detroit street in the late 1800s shows what was an undoubtedly noisy and bumpy ride upon unpaved streets.

Ambler House, and it may be truly said that much of the success of that place was due to her untiring efforts for the welfare of her guests."[5]

After William Ambler's death, the Ambler House was sold to Jabin Elliott in 1869. What was then known as the Elliott House became the scene of a victorious feast when the railroad finally came through Northville two years later. By 1889, the Elliott House had changed names again and was known as the Park House, having been purchased by O. Butler and his son. It was considered the leading hotel in town, noted for its fine cuisine and well-stocked bar. In 1893, the hotel was put on the market once more and was purchased by William Thurtle, a Bay City entrepreneur. A retired lumberman, Thurtle had also purchased the Northville Opera House a month earlier. When the telephone came to Northville, Thurtle's Park House was among the first to subscribe for the service in 1897.

In its day, the Park House was touted as "the best $2 per day house in Michigan." It was considered a truly outstanding hotel. In 1929, it stood as the oldest landmark of the village when it was totally destroyed by fire. At the time of the fire, the establishment was known as the Northville Hotel and Café, and it was owned by Edward Shafer. The furnishings were jointly owned by Peros and Peter Kartsonas and the *Northville Record* reported their loss as "a severe one, as they have been unable to get insurance on their goods." Shafer had only shortly before the inferno "secured a $5,000 policy on the building."[6]

Towards the end of the Civil War, the stagecoach was fast becoming obsolete, despite its revival in the Western states as part of the Pony Express Mail Service. By 1831, the first street railway in the country was inaugurated with the New York & Harlem Railroad Company in New York City. The coach was fitted with cast-iron wheels that rode on rails set in the road. Still pulled by horses, these railway cars were extremely popular and encouraged further development of the innovation. By 1850, the need for public transportation was greater than ever. More railway lines were added to New York City streets and other cities began to follow in their path. Boston began a railway line in 1856 and, by offering free rides, accommodated up to an amazing 2,000 passengers a day. Over the next few years, other cities joined the ranks of public railway service, including Philadelphia, Baltimore, Pittsburgh, Cincinnati, and Chicago.

The first horse-drawn streetcars appeared in Detroit in the summer of 1863. Operated by the newly-formed Detroit City Railway Company, the cars ran on rails laid along the streets. Horsecars plied Detroit's streets for the next 30 years. In November 1895, the last horsecar made its run, in favor of new technology. Horses, though sufficient for hauling heavy streetcars, were expensive to maintain and wore out quickly. They suffered from numerous ailments—mostly resulting from the heavy loads and severe weather conditions—and most were not able to survive more than three to five years of service.

Rapid technology during the Civil War helped improve the railroad system nationwide. By the late 1860s, travelers were discovering a more pleasing alternative to the swaying carriages and furrowed roads of the stagecoach. This change in style of travel brought an end to one era in American transportation, while another was just waiting to begin.

Railroads came to Michigan long before the Civil War began. As early as 1838, the Detroit & Pontiac Railroad and the Michigan Central Railroad served both eastern and western Michigan all the way to Kalamazoo.

Though prosperity and progress brought about advances in the railroad industry, there were many people who were unhappy with this new way of life. In the late 1840s, a series of private wars raged between some Detroiters and the railroad. Indignant farmers, angered by the slaughter of their cattle wandering in front of the engines, demanded the removal of the railroad; others tore up the tracks to keep the monster out of sight. Still more embittered citizens set fire to the new Michigan Central Depot in Detroit in 1850. Known as "the Great Conspiracy," this infamous court case caused a sensation in the city for many years. As trains continued to improve and gain speed, the loss of livestock to Detroit farmers was becoming too much to bear. Fences were constructed by the railroad, but the farmers were still considered responsible for their own stock, and ill will ran high. The crisis came to a head with the destruction of the three-year-old train station and all its contents, at a loss of $80,000. About a dozen perpetrators were arrested, taken to trial and found guilty, thus ending one of Detroit's most controversial issues of the nineteenth century.

Despite the trouble that went on in the state for years, the railroad pushed through until the line from Detroit to Chicago was opened in 1852. Before railroad depots were built, trains would stop anywhere along the route to service passengers. Unscheduled stops, whether to pick up passengers or even non-train–related errands by crew members, increased the need for permanent stations. Railroad depots were built in nearly every town in Michigan. Many towns existed originally because of the trains, while others prospered because of them.

Northville's railroad station originally stood on the west side of the tracks along Northville Road. In 1892, the citizens of Northville requested the Flint & Pere Marquette Railroad to construct a new depot to replace the old station that had been in use for the past 20 years. Around 1900, the depot was moved northeast of where the well stands today

The Northville Railroad Depot was originally built on the west side of the tracks, as seen in this early photo. (NHS.)

South Lyon's Witch's Hat Railroad Depot, built in 1909, replaced the original 1871 depot that burned in 1908. Moved to its current site at McHattie Park in South Lyon in 1976, the Queen Ann–style depot became a museum and community center in 1981. (Popkin.)

on Northville Road. In *Northville: The First Hundred Years*, author Jack Hoffman explains, "At the same time the depot was moved, the tracks themselves and the depot site were raised considerably to lessen the steep grade between here and Plymouth."[7]

The year 1871 saw the beginning of several area depots. The opening of Northville's first railroad station in June was cause for quite a celebration. The *Northville Record* looked forward to the event with eager anticipation. "The long looked-for Iron Horse will make its appearance at our Depot, accompanied by a retinue of coaches," it wrote. When the day arrived, the paper described the scene in excited detail: "the people from the entire country were about, and representatives from Pontiac, Clarkston, Milford, Lyon, Walled Lake, Detroit, Ypsilanti, Novi, Salem, and other places were making their appearance 'till our crowded streets assumed an aspect of seldom if ever witnessed in the history of our town."[8]

The festivities ended with the Northville Cornet Band leading the honored railroad employees to a special supper held at the Elliott House. Reported to be a "handsome" structure, the depot stood 102 feet long by 28 feet wide. The waiting rooms and ticket office were located in the north end of the building, while the freight department was situated in the south end.

"The Witch's Hat" is a romantic name describing South Lyon's most unusual feature: the old railroad station-turned historical museum. The depot was a focal point in the village when it was built in 1909 and remains so to this day. With its steeply-peaked black roof, the building does indeed resemble a witch's hat. The Pere Marquette Railway Depot in Novi was built along the tracks below Grand River Road. Designed strictly for utilitarian purposes, the long wooden building serviced many Novi residents over the years. The railroad station was an important feature of any town, regardless of its size. Having a train station in one's town was an indication of status, a symbol of progress, and a sign that prosperity was indeed in the near future.

Two forms of locomotion are seen in this early 1900s postcard. The train traveled through Northville, as did the interurban, crossing just below it.

The railroad proved to be an expedient alternative to the slow-moving stagecoaches. It provided efficient transportation for Northville residents and supplies making their way to other parts of the state. For the first time, residents of Northville were connected physically with the rest of the world—at least the eastern half of the United States and Canada.

In 1869, the Michigan Central offered four express trains daily between Detroit and Chicago. "Pullman's Palace Sleeping Cars" were featured on all-night trains; ladies had their own cars on all-day trains. Patented by George Pullman of Chicago, the sleeping car was a magnificent innovation for passengers on long overnight train trips. In October 1865, the *Detroit Free Press* excitedly described the smooth ride, the elegant exterior, and luxurious interior, plus the comfortable conditions of the car in some detail: "For the purpose for which it was built," it raved, "this car excells [*sic*] anything we have yet seen on any road, east or west."[9]

Other lines also served the Novi-Northville area in 1869. The Grand Trunk Railroad left Detroit daily (except Sundays) for eastern Canada to Montreal, New York, and New England. This line advertised "passenger fare lower than via any other route." In the same year the Jackson, Lansing & Saginaw Railroad took travelers north as far as Saginaw. The train stopped in Northville all the way up into the 1950s.

Railroads held the country together, connecting coast to coast. Still considered vital to the national economy, trains continue to clatter along tracks through Northville, bringing the sounds of history into our lives daily.

Public transportation in Detroit came in many forms throughout the late nineteenth and early twentieth centuries. Among the most colorful was the electric interurban. The interurban, or electric streetcar, was a combination of the earlier horsecar and modern technology. More comfortable than the horsecar, more convenient than the railroad, the interurban sailed through Detroit and its environs for many years. Gaining speeds of up to 60 miles per hour, the interurban was a popular form of transportation that carried passengers as far as 75 miles from Detroit in many directions.

After the Civil War ended in 1865, more people began to migrate to the cities. The Industrial Revolution that resulted from the war produced factory jobs that were more reliable than the seasonal farm work had been. Young men and their families began a gradual but steady flow away from the farms. As more and more people began to move to the cities, the demand for fresh farm produce rose. The highly efficient interurban lines provided an inexpensive and expedient way to ship farm goods to their urban destinations. By the time the interurban came to Northville in the late 1890s, Detroit was reportedly labeled as the "interurban capital of America." More lines traveled out of Detroit than from any other city.

The electric streetcar was a phenomenal success and independent line owners rivaled for service. The Detroit, Ypsilanti, and Ann Arbor line was the first company to approach Northville with a proposed route in 1898. Their lines promised hourly service to and from Plymouth, which connected with the cities of Wayne and Detroit at low rates. Soon, however, the Detroit, Pike's Peak and Ann Arbor Railway offered a similar plan along a different route. This line also included the transportation of milk from farmers, along with the passenger cars.

Instead of going with either line, however, Northville joined with Detroit and Plymouth in September 1898, to incorporate the Detroit, Plymouth & Northville Electric Railway Company (DP&N). Disputes and disagreements eventually resulted in a name change to the Detroit and Northwestern Railway Co. The interurban finally made its debut in Northville in November 1899, with a train arriving from Plymouth. Soon, a second line was added and interurban service in Northville was being handled by two separate companies. The Detroit United Railway (DUR) consolidated all the various independent interurban lines in 1901. The DP&N became a branch line of the DUR. The lines grew to encompass much of the state, enabling Northville and Novi residents to travel, via Farmington, as far as Toledo, Ohio, or Kalamazoo and Grand Rapids.

Besides providing transportation, the interurban also ended up furnishing streetlights for a number of communities along the route, including Northville, Farmington, and Plymouth. Northville's stipulation in its contract with the DUR required three streetlights each between Bradner and Northville Roads. According to historian Jack Schramm, "This provision was amended in 1904 to add lights at Benton's and Wiltsey's crossings."[10] The next year Northville requested even more lights, to be placed at each street crossing on the line.

When the first car came to Northville in the fall of 1899, fares were 10¢ from Plymouth to Northville and 15¢ from Plymouth to Wayne. The Wayne station was one of the busiest on the entire line. Trains ran once an hour, beginning at 6:15 a.m. until 11:15 p.m. From Wayne, one could transfer to a train going either to Detroit or to Ypsilanti and Ann Arbor. Return trips from Detroit's City Hall also left regularly up to nine o'clock p.m., with the connection at Wayne. Travel time between Northville and Detroit, including the transfer at Wayne, was approximately two and a half hours. The waiting room for the DP&N interurban was located on the west side of Center Street.

141

Northville's DUR Express Office was located near the Union Manufacturing & Lumber Company at the corner of Main and Griswold Streets. This 1908 photo shows farmers taking their produce to the streetcar depot. (NHS.)

The Wayne-Northville DUR line was cut back in the 1920s. Also cut was the Northville-Farmington route, which had continued into Redford. Bankruptcy court ordered the abandonment of the line, and by 1928 the DUR to Northville had ended. The life of the interurban spanned almost four decades. By the 1920s, new modes of public transit, such as busses, which were far less expensive to run, had pushed the romantic interurbans into obsolescence. The end of the interurban in Northville was greeted with sadness by many residents.

Though it can take just over a half-hour to get into the city of Detroit these days, Northville residents are limited by one thing: to get anywhere, one has to drive. Bus service was, though slow, a convenient way of getting to Detroit or Ann Arbor in earlier years, after the DUR service ended.

In 1922, the City of Detroit's Department of Street Railways (DSR) had begun the municipal ownership and operation of all street railways within the city limits. Detroit thus became the first city in the nation to find an alternative to privately-owned mass transit. The demise of the rail service came with the paving of the roads, and bus service replaced the abandoned rail lines in the 1920s. With the paving of Northville Road to Plymouth in 1922, bus service was made possible. The Detroit Motorbus Company in 1925 began service from Detroit directly to Plymouth and Northville. The routes ran via Plymouth Road and via Seven Mile Road. According to Schramm, "Those direct routes were not only faster, but eliminated the transfer at Wayne. After this service started, DUR's rail branch was doomed."[11]

By the 1960s, when DSR busses began an extended run to Livonia Mall along Grand River Avenue, a conflict arose with a private bus company out of Northville. The Northville Coach Lines provided a limited service to the mall. They took the DSR to court, claiming the extended service to the suburbs (*i.e.* Redford Township and Livonia) was cutting in on their territory. Northville Coach Lines lost the suit in Circuit Court and the DSR continued its service to Livonia Mall for many years. While freight trains still race through Northville daily, there are no longer any stops in town, and passenger train and bus services were discontinued long ago.

From horseback to stagecoach to the railroad, Americans had been searching for the ideal mode of transportation. In the late 1800s, they found it. Railroads may have connected one end of the United States to the other, but it was the automobile that really put America on the road.

The first gasoline-driven automobile seen on the streets of Detroit was Charles B. King's four-cylinder vehicle in 1896. Looking more like a horse-drawn buggy than a motorized contraption of the future, the car had high iron tires, with the engine located beneath the seat rather than under a hood. The *Detroit Free Press* was not especially impressed with the demonstration: "The first horseless carriage seen in this city was out on the streets last night," went the report of March 7, 1896. "The apparatus seemed to work all right, and it went at the rate of five or six miles an hour at an even rate of speed."

Though the newspaper may not have been excited by its appearance, other local inventors raced to join the auto bandwagon. Henry Ford came out with his first automobile in Detroit in June 1896, and Ransom E. Olds began his Motor Vehicle Company a year later in Lansing.

The automobile soon became a national sensation. In 1900, there were 8,000 cars registered in the United States; just five years later, the number jumped incredibly to over 70,000 registered automobiles in the country.

The automobile continued to progress, and with its evolution came inevitable changes in the American way of life. A cry for better roads was heard from coast to coast, and rutted

Just south of the city of Northville, the interurban passes by the Stimpson Scale Manufacturing Company plant.

dirt trails began to receive national attention. In 1904, a survey was taken of American roads, and it was discovered that—give or take a few miles—there were over 2,000,000 miles of roads in the nation. By 1915, there were nearly as many registered automobiles as there were miles of roads in the country, and the U.S. Congress realized the need for improvements. The Federal Highway Act was passed in 1921, and since then the construction and maintenance of the nation's roads have been under governmental supervision. The automobile clearly changed the lives of Americans in the twentieth century, from beginning as a novel plaything in the 1920s to a vital force in the modern way of life.

Displaying, buying, and selling automobiles also became a way of life beginning in the early twentieth century. Though it may seem like an innately American institution, the auto show actually had foreign origins. The world's first auto show was held in England in 1895. A Detroit bicycle dealer who attended the exhibit was so impressed and inspired by the innovation, that he came home with plans to exhibit cars in his own country. William E. Metzger not only organized Detroit's first auto show, but he also opened the first car dealership in the city. With his business partner, Metzger created the Tri-State Sportsman's and Automobile Association in 1899, and the group began to display sporting goods, bicycles, and a few automobiles. This went on for some time, with autos taking second place to the more popular bicycles.

The popularity of the automobiles in the exhibits necessitated the creation of an organizing body; the Detroit Auto Dealers' Association (DADA) was born. The new association was a success from the start, and Detroit's first auto show opened in 1901. By 1907, the show began to display what the Motor City would become, with Detroit cars being shown by Detroit dealers for the first time. The location of the 1907 show was Riverview Park, near Belle Isle at Grand Boulevard in Detroit. It was at this exhibit that gasoline cars were displayed along with electric and steam cars as well.

An early automobile is seen driving across the Northville bridge near the town's manufacturing district in 1927.

During the second half of the nineteenth century, about 60 patents were issued for various forms of motor transportation. These varied from engines run by ammonia, coal, and steam, before gasoline was introduced in 1891 by the Duryea brothers. Electric vehicles were first patented in 1895 by Morris & Salon, but both steam and electric-powered cars were overshadowed by the more successful gasoline engines. R.E. Olds was one of the pioneers in developing a gasoline vehicle; his automobile factory became Michigan's first such company in 1897.

Though the first electric vehicle was built in 1836, they didn't gain popularity until the end of the nineteenth and early twentieth centuries. The electric car industry had its peak year in 1912, when 34,000 vehicles were registered with American owners. In 1913, when the Edison Storage Battery Company was in financial trouble, Thomas Edison suggested to his friend Henry Ford that he develop a battery-powered automobile. With the idea that both men would become successful by the project, they unfortunately discovered that the new cars were too heavy, too slow, and too expensive to produce. By 1915, the project had ended.

The 1920s saw the beginning of the end of the electric car craze. With new, cheaper gasoline technology, the electric car soon became a thing of the past. By the late 1920s, hundreds of thousands of spectators were streaming to the auto shows, but the shows by that time were pretty much confined to gasoline-driven vehicles.

The 1910 Detroit Auto Show was remarkable in that it showed cars with their equipment attached. That is, windshield wipers, headlights, and other important "extras" were—for the first time—provided with the purchase price of the car.

The location of the auto shows varied from year to year, until 1924, when a Convention Hall was built at Woodward and Canfield. This remained the site of the Detroit show for the next 16 years. World War II halted not only car production, but the auto show as well. It was, in fact, postponed for over a decade. The 41st Detroit Auto Show was finally held in February 1954, with record-breaking attendance. Nearly 50,000 people braved the cold, rainy weather to troop to the Michigan State Fairgrounds the first day alone. Every year since then, the shows have continued to get bigger and better. The Detroit Auto Show became the North American International Auto Show in 1989, the year more foreign models were introduced. When Cobo Hall was completed in 1960, the auto show had found its home, and has been there ever since.

Though Detroit is the place to be for the auto show today, in the 1920s, at least, it was not the only show in town. In September 1929, the *Northville Record* reported that the auto show at the Northville–Wayne County Fair was to be a "big feature" of the festivities, with "more cars . . . exhibited this year than ever before." The *Record* predicted that the 1929 showing would be "the finest auto exhibit ever shown on the fairgrounds." Over 50 new models were on display in the main tent, with nearly every area car dealer showing up to exhibit his latest models. Dayton Bunn, a Northville Ford dealer, was noted to have the largest display, with ten new cars.

The Northville auto show was a well-attended event, and one that kept both visitors and dealers happy. The *Record* wrote, "In spite of the disagreeable weather in previous years, dealers have always been able to make enough sales to make the event worthwhile."[12]

The invention of the automobile, and its subsequent popularity, brought about a need for how to keep it going. Before gas stations came into being, refueling one's motor car was a tricky, time-consuming process. Gasoline itself was only available at certain locations—which could tend to be few and far between—and required considerable planning on the part of the driver in order to obtain it.

The world's first service station opened in Bordeaux, France, in 1895. Two years later, a station opened in Great Britain, but the most important improvements came from America. In 1905, the Automobile Gasoline Company, founded in St. Louis, Missouri, came out with a method of storing gasoline in bulk. Bulk depot outlets contained large containers which held the fuel. A small pitcher was used to transfer the gasoline from the large tank and it was funneled into the car's tank. It was a time-consuming, messy, and often dangerous procedure that could take up to three men to manipulate all the moving parts.

As more cars began to hit the streets, the bulk depots became even more unwieldy, and smaller, one-gallon containers started to be sold to motorists. This way, they could purchase fuel ahead of time in preparation for its use, but there was still the problem of transferring the gas from container to car. The Automobile Gasoline Co. came up with a clever yet simple idea to perfect this problem. Gasoline was dispensed through an ordinary garden hose that was connected to a gravity-fed tank. The hose did away with the funnel, making it easier to fill one's tank.

The first pump was invented by S.F. Bowser of Fort Wayne, Indiana, in 1885, but it did not originally deal with the auto industry. A Fort Wayne storekeeper approached inventor Bowser for a creation that would keep his leaky kerosene barrel from contaminating his nearby butter barrel. Instead of simply separating the two containers to different parts of the store, Bowser created a method of dispensing the lamp oil in specific quantities, thereby eliminating the leakage and keeping customers happy. Using the same idea for the distribution of motor fuel did not catch on until 20 years later, but it was S.F. Bowser and Co. who came up with the patent for it. He was also responsible for a device to measure how much fuel was being dispensed, in 1925, and a pump to automatically record the price of the gas being pumped into the vehicle, in 1932.

Early gas stations often consisted of a small wooden building and a free-standing pump. The traditional form of the gas station, with its projecting canopy still in use today, was first seen at a Standard Oil station in Seattle in 1907.

"Northville's Only Full-Service Station" is a sign proudly displayed in the window of Asher's Citgo Station. Located in Northville since 1951, Asher's brings customers into a bygone era of friendly gas station attendants who not only pump gas, but clean windshields and check the oil as part of their regular service.

Once Northville boasted over a dozen full-serve gas stations; now there is only one. Asher's gas station celebrated its 50th year in Northville on February 1, 2001. Back in the 1950s, when it was built, there were at least 14 gas stations and 3 car dealerships to contend with. Bill Asher, original owner of the station, said, "You fought for everything you got," with all the competition in the area. "There was a forty-seven percent failure rate," he explained. "Guys kept fading away, fading away." Four self-service stations are left in the Northville; Asher's has survived as the last full-serve.

Three generations of the Asher family are represented here; they are, from left to right, as follows: Bill (original owner), grandsons Chris and Mathew, and son Rick (current owner). The station has been located on Fairbrook and Rogers Streets since 1957. (Popkin.)

Born in the Thumb area of Michigan, Asher moved to Northville with his parents in 1941. While attending Northville High School for the 11th and 12th grades, he met his future wife, the former Margie Sessions, a Northville native. After coming home from serving in World War II, Asher went to work for Ford Motor Company. He also worked part-time at a gas station and found he preferred the latter job, so he decided to go into business for himself. In 1951, at age 26, he went into a partnership with Julius Feole, and the two men opened a gas station at Main and Wing Streets.

At the time Asher's first station opened, it was a Hi-Speed station. Hi-Speed gasoline was owned by the Hickok Oil Company, which dealt mainly with Detroit, Toledo, and Cleveland stations. Pure Oil eventually took over the Hi-Speed companies in order to strengthen its Northern and Southern markets, and Asher's Hi-Speed became Asher's Pure. They stayed with this company through the 1970s, when the station changed to Union 76. This company was Bill Asher's favorite. "I hated to see them go," he lamented, "because they were a good company and they were good to me." But when they pulled out of Michigan, Asher's was forced to change names again, and in the 1990s, it became Asher's Citgo.

Northville's skies have been the scenes of many curious events over the years. On one notable day in 1932, airplanes were seen to swoop in deep circles high overhead. They symbolized the mourning being held for one of aviation's most famous heroes. Eddie Stinson, known as "the dean of American aviators," was a nationally known leader in the field who had an aircraft manufacturing company in Northville in the late 1920s.

Coming from a high-flying family, Stinson first learned to fly from his older sister, Katherine, reportedly the second woman ever to fly a plane. She was quite a celebrity in her own right. At the age of 16, in 1912, Katherine received her pilot's license and went on to become one of the great performers and inventors of stunt flying. She was a woman of firsts: she was the first woman to practice skywriting, the first to carry airmail for the U.S. Postal Service, and the first woman pilot in the Far East. Katherine set an endurance record in 1918, flying non-stop from San Diego to San Francisco, a distance of over 600 miles.

Another sister, Marjorie, became a plane designer for the U.S. Navy. Early in their careers, the Stinson family, along with brother Jack and their mother, set up a flying school in Texas. Eddie went on to establish himself, as had his sister before him, as a leading record-breaker. In 1927, Eddie Stinson became president of the Stinson Aircraft Corp. in Northville. The landing strip was located near Beck Road and Six Mile.

One of his planes, the Stinson Detroiter, set a world's duration record of over 50 hours, 36 minutes. This plane was one of the first mail planes converted for passenger use. It was purchased by Northwest Airlines, serving well into the 1930s. Stinson's record-breaking products contributed considerably to his company's success. "Business at the Stinson plant," wrote the *Northville Record* in 1928, "has for some time past been assuming rush proportions," and the coming year's production was predicted to be at least four times greater than that of the previous year.[13]

Eddie Stinson became known as the "Dean of American aviators." His aircraft manufacturing company was located in Northville in the late 1920s.

Seen here in this 1927 photograph, the Stinson Aircraft Factory was located in Northville's manufacturing district.

Stinson set a new speed record on February 21, 1928, while delivering one of his planes to a customer in Syracuse, New York. The average speed of his monoplane was 161 miles per hour during the 410-mile flight. Making the trip from Northville to Syracuse in 2 hours, 32 minutes, Stinson cut 28 minutes off an earlier record.

One of Stinson's aircraft was also the scene of one of the most unusual wedding ceremonies. Unwilling to wait for Michigan's required five days between the application of a marriage license and the date of the wedding, a local couple made other plans. Helen M. Hovey, age 25, a musician, and Jack Whittacker, 32, a vice president of the Szekeley Aircraft Co. of Holland, Michigan, called on Stinson to solve their dilemma. Reverend William Richard of the Methodist church was recruited to perform the ceremony. Other passengers included Stinson and his wife, Estelle; Stinson Company pilot Randolph G. Page; and Lou Firsht, Whittacker's former secretary. The adventurous group flew to Toledo to obtain an Ohio marriage license, which did not have any waiting requirements. High above the Toledo Transcontinental Airport, in Ohio airspace, the couple said their vows. "Instead of the customary tin cans and shoes that decorate wedding vehicles," a Toledo newspaper reported, "the honeymoon plane was covered with signs such as 'Atta girl, Helen' and 'We're just married.' "[14]

Eddie Stinson died on January 26, 1932 in an airplane crash in Chicago. Aviation was his life, and he is still remembered as one of the great pioneers in the field.

From muddy stagecoach trails to Eddie Stinson's record-breaking flights, improvements in travel have helped push Northville into the mainstream, connecting it with the major cities within the state and the country.

EPILOGUE

There is an old *Twilight Zone* episode in which an extremely stressed-out office worker gets on his homeward-bound train and discovers an idyllic stop known as "Willoughby," a village eternally locked in the summer of 1880. What was merely a dream for the overworked city executive, a place in another century can actually be found in many communities around the country and almost in our own backyards.

Henry Ford started it all. In 1923, Ford purchased 2,600 acres of land near South Sudbury, Massachusetts. The Wayside Inn, dating from 1686, was the nucleus of this first historical village in the United States. By preserving the ancient inn, Ford also saved numerous neighboring buildings and brought to America the idea of "participatory history," in which one could—literally—walk in the footsteps of our country's forefathers. One year later, he brought his idea to Michigan with the purchase of the 1836 Botsford Inn. A traditional way-station along the Grand River Road, this well-used tavern still survives today as a monument to historic preservation. Ford's third and most demanding undertaking was an outgrowth of these two earlier projects. Creating a village dedicated to early American life became a reality in 1929. Greenfield Village, located in Dearborn, remains among the gems of historic villages in the United States.

Meanwhile, other such villages sprang up across the country, including a couple very close to home. On the corner of Eight Mile and Newburgh Roads sits another open-air museum, known as Greenmead, or the Livonia Historical Village. The focal point of Livonia's Greenmead is the stately Greek-revival home located amid the lush meadows that gave the estate its name. The home was built in 1841 by Joshua Simmons, who came to Livonia from New York in 1826.

His son, Richmond, later moved to Novi, where his orchard gained wide recognition. Members of the Joshua Simmons family lived on the Livonia homestead into the twentieth century. It was sold in 1919 to attorney Sherwin Hill and his wife, who restored the estate to its former elegance. It remained in the Hill family for over 50 years. In 1976, the City of Livonia purchased the property and began to turn the area into a historical village. Calling the home the Hill House Museum, in honor of Mrs. Hill, the park has

Northville's Mill Race Historical Village, located on property donated by the Ford Motor Company and established in 1972, is operated by the Northville Historical Society. (Popkin.)

grown since then to include a church and a one-room schoolhouse among its more than one dozen structures.

Henry Ford was indirectly responsible for the creation of Northville's Mill Race Historical Village. It was the Ford Motor Company's gift of 11 acres of land to the City of Northville in 1972, specifically designated for the creation of a historical village and park, that led to the current "Willoughby" imitation. Like Livonia's Greenmead, Northville's Mill Race Village is a combination park, gardens, museum, and historic village dedicated to preserving a taste of a long-past era. By the year 2000, Mill Race Village contained seven original structures, plus a reproduction working blacksmith shop and an ornamental gazebo.

Located on the picturesque Mill Pond, the village was once the core of Northville's business community, with a number of mills situated at this site over the years. In the early nineteenth century, most mills, such as sawmills or gristmills that were powered by waterwheels, depended upon a canal or channel of water known as a "raceway" or simply "race." By definition, a millrace is a canal in which water flows to and from a mill wheel. Though the mill has long since faded into history, its memory is kept alive with Mill Race Historical Village.

The most imposing of the structures is the New School Church. Built in 1845 in the Greek Revival style, it was actually used as a church for only the first four years of its existence. It served for over 70 years as the Northville Public Library, in between other purposes ranging from school to opera house to township hall.

The Wash-Oak School, built in 1873, was moved to Mill Race Village in 1975. Today, the building has been restored to the style of the late nineteenth century. Black slate paint was used on the walls for blackboards; reproduction desks were built in the style of student desks of the period, including the use of square-headed nails. Today, countless children from area schools are able to visit and spend the day imagining what life was like in an earlier time.

151

The Hunter House is a Greek revival-style home that was built around 1849 by Stephen and Mary Hunter. They had come to Michigan in the 1840s, settling in Northville where Hunter worked as a miller. Their house is restored to reflect the type of furnishings typically used by a working-class family of this time.

Standing slightly apart from the other buildings, exuding an aura of stately elegance, is the Yerkes House. This Victorian masterpiece was built in 1868 for William and Sarah Yerkes. Yerkes was a judge who became the first president of the Village of Northville. His wealth and prestige are reflected in his home. The furnishings depict the typical ornate Victorian style, which reached its height of popularity in the mid-nineteenth century.

Gleaming in its own Victorian splendor stands a gazebo, or bandstand, built for the village by high school shop students in 1979. It was patterned after an 1880-style "crow's nest" gazebo. A decorative cottage, known simply as the Cottage House, was built in the 1890s in the Victorian style. It is now used as a studio for the Mill Race Weaver's Guild. A blacksmith shop, completed in 1985, also houses the village store. The stone building was designed as a working forge, providing visitors with actual examples of that ancient craft.

The Cady Inn was moved to the village in 1987. The two-story, saltbox-style structure is believed to date from about 1832. It was used at various times as a stagecoach stop, a tavern, and even a station of the Underground Railroad before and during the Civil War. It has been restored as an inn, but also houses the village offices and archives.

A turn-of-the-century interurban station was added to the village in 1993. Originally located at Eight Mile and Newburgh Roads, it served as a waiting room on the Northville-Pontiac interurban route from 1899 to 1929.

Like our *Twilight Zone* tale, taking a trip to an open-air museum can be like visiting "a lovely little village . . . You ought to try it sometime. Peaceful, restful, where a man can slow down to walk and live his life full measure."[1] That is the story of Northville, Michigan.

Constructed in 1979 by high school shop students, the Victorian-style gazebo provides a picturesque backdrop for many summer weddings in Northville. (Popkin.)

BIBLIOGRAPHY

BOOKS

Anderson, Dave. *The Story of Football*. New York: William Morrow & Co., 1985.

Bald, F. Clever. *Michigan in Four Centuries*. New York: Harper & Brothers, 1954.

Barfknecht, Gary. *Michellaneous*. Davison, Montana: Friede Publishers, 1982.

———. *Michellaneous II*. Davison, Montana: Friede Publishers, 1985.

Bingay, Malcolm. *Detroit Is My Own Home Town*. Indianapolis: Bobbs-Merrill Co., 1946.

Bowen, Dana Thomas. *Lore of the Lakes*. Daytona Beach, Florida: Dana Thomas Bowen Pub., 1940.

Buehr, Walter. *Home Sweet Home in the 19th Century*. New York: Thomas Y. Crowell Co., 1965.

Cole, Maurice. *Voices from the Wilderness*. Ann Arbor: Edward Brothers, 1961.

Dunbar, Willis Frederick. *Michigan: A History of the Wolverine State*. Grand Rapids: W.B. Eerdmans Pub. Co., 1965.

Durant, Samuel. *History of Oakland County, Michigan*. Philadelphia: Everts & Co., 1877.

Earle, Alice Morse. *Home Life in Colonial Days*. New York: The MacMillan Co., 1957.

Evans, Mary. *Costume through the Ages*. Philadelphia: J.B. Lippincott Co., 1950.

Hoffman, Jack. *Northville: The First Hundred Years*. Silver Springs Questers, 1976.

Jakle, John A. *The Gas Station in America*. Baltimore: John Hopkins University Press, 1994.

Kresge's Katalog. Detroit, 1913. Facsimile edition, 1975.

Louie, Barbara G. *No. VI on the Trail: A History of Novi, Michigan*. Novi, Michigan: Novi Historical Commission, 1991.

Louie, Barbara G., and Diane Rockall. *Step by Step through Northville: Four Walking Tours*. Northville Historical Society, 1989.

Michigan Manual. Department of Management and Budget, 1977–78; 1999–2000.

Michigan Pioneer and Historical Collections. Lansing: W.S. George & Co., 1877–1884 (Vols. 1–5).

Northville: The Ideal Suburban Village. 1892. Facsimile edition, 1974.

Reck, Franklin M. *The Romance of American Transportation*. New York: Crowell, 1962.

Rips, Rae Elizabeth, ed. *Detroit in Its World Setting: A 250-Year Chronology, 1701–1951*. Detroit: Detroit Public Library, 1953.

Robertson, Patrick. *The Book of Firsts*. New York: Bramhall House, 1982.

Schramm, Jack E., William H. Heming, and Richard R. Andrews. *When Eastern Michigan Rode the Rails, Book III*. Glendale, California: Interurban Press, 1988.

Schweitzer, Robert, and Michael Davis. *America's Favorite Homes: Mail-Order Catalogues as a Guide to Popular Early 20th-Century Houses*. Detroit: Wayne State University Press, 1990.

Sears, Roebuck and Co. Consumers Guide, Fall 1900. Northfield, Illinois: DBI Books, 1970.

Sloane, Eric. *Eric Sloane's America*. New York: Promotory Press, 1982.

Stevenson, Katherine Cole. *Houses by Mail: A Guide to Houses from Sears, Roebuck & Company*. Washington, D.C.: Preservation Press, 1986.

Wayne County Chronography. Detroit: Bornman & Co., 1890.

Wilson, Diane F. *Cornerstones: A History of Canton Township Families*. Canton: Canton Historical Society, 1984.

Witzel, Michael Karl. *The American Gas Station*. Osceola, Wisconsin: Motorbooks International, 1992.

NEWSPAPERS AND PERIODICALS

Boilio, Bob. "Village Industries." *Chronicle: The Magazine of the Historical Society of Michigan*. Winter 1982.

Burke, Philip E. "William Henry Maybury." *The Maybury Manual*. 1941.

Detroit Advertiser. 16 November 1850.

Detroit Advertiser & Tribune. 7 November 1867.

Detroit Free Press. 1849, 1860–62, 1865, 1892, 1923, 1931, 1941, 1949.

Detroit News. 1932, 1942, 1959.

Detroit Saturday Night. 1907.

Harmon, Frank S. *Northville Record*. 26 August 1927.

Little, Samuel H. *Northville Record*. 23 July 1870.

Michigan Christian Herald. 10 October 1850.

Northville Records. 1870–71, 1873, 1876–78, 1893, 1897–99, 1902, 1907, 1910, 1917, 1925, 1927–29, 1931, 1936, 1943, 1958.

Northville Record Centennial Edition. 17 July 1969.

Prevost, Clifford A. "Officials Live Like Monarchs at Northville." *Detroit Free Press*. 28 July 1932.

Scientific American. 28 August 1945.

Sudomier, William. "Northville Stays Up All Night." *Detroit Free Press*. 30 May 1957.

Thompson, C.L. "Northville Labs Make Vanilla." *Detroit Times*. 15 September 1935.

Tschirhart, Don. "Northville Clerk Recalls Old Days." *Detroit News*. 14 November 1959.

Varnum, Mina Humphries. *Detroit Saturday Night*. 1927.

Wayne County Record. 1869

Yerkes, Robert. "Early History of Novi Town." *Northville Record*. 20 October 1899; 27 October 1899; 3 November 1899.

MANUSCRIPTS

The primary sources used for this book are all found in the manuscript collection of the Burton Historical Collection, Detroit Public Library.

Allen, John.

Banks, Sarah Gertrude.

Clarkson, David.

Herriman, Daniel.

Michigan Historical Society Papers, 1829–1881.

Sackett family papers.

Sheldon, John Pitts.

UNPUBLISHED AND MISCELLANEOUS SOURCES

Asher, William. Interview. Northville, Michigan. 22 January 2001.

Darga, Nancy. Telephone interview. August 2000.

Davis, Michael. "Early 20th Century Catalog Houses." Lecture. Wayne State University Local History Conference. Detroit, 1990.

A History of Northville. Unpublished manuscript written by the eighth-grade social studies classes, Northville Public Schools, 1954.

Williamson, Daniel R. "The Samuel White Family before and after They Arrived in Novi, Michigan." Unpublished manuscript. June 1988.

The city's police station, located in what was once the Northville Public Library, is part of City Hall on Main Street. (Popkin.)

ENDNOTES

CHAPTER ONE

1. Durant, Samuel. *History of Oakland County, Michigan*. p. 231.
2. Williamson, Daniel R. "The Samuel White Family before and after They Arrived in Novi, Michigan." Unpublished manuscript, June 1988.
3. Clarkson, David. "Pioneer Manuscripts." Burton Historical Collection, Detroit Public Library.
4. "Excursion to Macinac." *Northville Record*. 6 August 1870.
5. *Michigan Pioneer & Historical Collections* (1894–95): Vol. 26, p. 493.
6. *Wayne County Chronography*. pp. 134–135.
7. *Northville Record*. 1897.
8. *Detroit Free Press*. 31 January 1892.

CHAPTER TWO

1. Durant, Samuel. *History of Oakland County, Michigan*. p. 68.
2. Utley, Henry. *Michigan Pioneer & Historical Collections*. Vol. 1, p. 446.
3. Durant, Samuel. *History of Oakland County, Michigan*. p. 217.
4. *Northville Record*. 10 May 1873.
5. Michigan Historical Society Papers, 1829–1881. Burton Historical Collection, Detroit Public Library.
6. Wilson, Diane F. *Cornerstones: A History of Canton Township Families*. p. 521.
7. Sheldon, John Pitts. Burton Historical Collection, Detroit Public Library.
8. *Northville Record*.

CHAPTER THREE

1. *Michigan Pioneer & Historical Collections* (1881): Vol. 4, p. 421.
2. Banks, Sarah Gertrude. Burton Historical Collection, Detroit Public Library.
3. "What a Librarian Is Paid." *Northville Record*. 22 February 1929.

CHAPTER FOUR

1. Stebbins, C.B. *Michigan Pioneer & Historical Collections* (1882): Vol. 5, pp. 131–132.
2. Clarkson, David. "Pioneer Sketches." Burton Historical Collection, Detroit Public Library.
3. "A Grand Success." *Northville Record.* 4 August 1893.
4. Burke, Philip E. "William Henry Maybury." *The Maybury Manual.* p. 6.
5. *Scientific American.* 28 August 1845.
6. *Detroit Free Press.* 30 September 1860.
7. Ibid.
8. Harmon, Frank S. *Northville Record.* 26 August 1927.
9. *Detroit News.*
10. *Northville: The Ideal Suburban Village.* (unpaged).

CHAPTER FIVE

1. Clarkson, David. "Pioneer Sketches." Burton Historical Collection, Detroit Public Library.
2. Williams, B.O. *Michigan Pioneer & Historical Collections* (1882): Vol. 5, p. 547.
3. Yerkes, Robert. "Early History of Novi Town." *Northville Record.* 20 and 27 October 1899.
4. "Just Half a Dozen." *Northville Record.* April 1893.
5. "Experts Visit Morons Home." *Detroit Free Press.* June 1923.
6. Ibid.
7. "Amazing Handicraft Shown by Handicapped Children." *Detroit News.* 8 April 1932.
8. Pollard, Donald. "Human Wrecks Salvaged by Wayne Training School." *Detroit News.* 2 October 1932.
9. Cole, Maurice. *Voices from the Wilderness.* pp. 220–221.
10. Ibid., pp. 33, 35.
11. Clarkson, David. "Pioneer Sketches." Burton Historical Collection, Detroit Public Library.
12. *Northville Record.*
13. *Northville Record.* 26 September 1902.

CHAPTER SIX

1. *Michigan Christian Herald.* 10 October 1850.
2. *Detroit Advertiser.* 16 November 1850.
3. Sackett family papers. Burton Historical Collection, Detroit Public Library.
4. Herriman, Daniel. Burton Historical Collection, Detroit Public Library.
5. Ibid.

CHAPTER SEVEN

1. Clarkson, David. "Pioneer Sketches." Burton Historical Collection, Detroit Public Library.
2. *Northville Record Centennial Edition.* 17 July 1969; 3E.
3. Boelio, Bob. "Village Industries." *Chronicle: The Magazine of the Historical Society of Michigan.* Winter 1982. pp. 36–40.
4. *Northville: The Ideal Suburban Village.* (unpaged).
5. "Gordon Baking Company Has Large Capacity at Condensed Milk Plant." *Northville Record.* 12 June 1931.
6. Ibid.

7. Harmon, Frank. *Northville Record*. 26 August 1927.

8. *Northville Record*. 12 June 1931.

9. "New Market." *Northville Record*. 7 July 1893.

10. *Northville Record*. 13 October 1893.

11. "Clock Stopped by Ice Storm." *Northville Record*. 1 February 1929.

12. Davis, Michael. "Early 20th Century Catalogue Houses." Lecture. 1990.

13. Thompson, C.L. "Northville Labs Make Vanilla." *Detroit Times*. 15 September 1935.

14. Ibid.

15. Thomas, Ella. "Wrecking of Northville Site Recalls Old Days." *Detroit Free Press*. 19 April 1931.

16. Ibid.

CHAPTER EIGHT

1. Clarkson, David. "Pioneer Sketches." Burton Historical Collection, Detroit Public Library.

2. John Allen manuscript. Burton Historical Collection, Detroit Public Library.

3. Little, Samuel. *Northville Record*. 23 July 1870.

4. *Northville Record*. 4 March 1898.

5. *Northville Record*. 17 July 1958.

CHAPTER NINE

1. *Northville Record*. 19 August 1893.

2. *Northville Record*. 1893.

3. "The Foot Race." *Northville Record*. 21 October 1876.

4. *Detroit Advertiser & Tribune*. 7 November 1867.

5. Ibid.

6. "Horse Race." *Wayne County Record*. 23 October 1869.

7. *A History of Northville*. Unpublished manuscript. p. 21.

8. *Northville Record*. 1 April 1910.

9. Ibid.

10. *Detroit Free Press*. 13 February 1862.

11. Ibid.

12. "Base Ball." *Northville Record*. 14 July 1876.

13. "Dehoco Defeats Lansing Oil Team." *Northville Record*. 14 June 1929.

14. *Northville Record*. 1898.

15. "Plymouth Is Vanquished by High Team." *Northville Record*. 8 November 1929.

16. Varnum, Mina Humphries. *Detroit Saturday Night*. 1927.

17. Darga, Nancy. Interview. August 2000.

18. "The 4th at Plymouth." *Northville Record*. 7 July 1893.

19. *Wayne County Record*. 25 September 1869.

20. *Northville Record*. 16 June 1877.

21. Callaghan, J. Dorsey. "Last Reception before Arrival of Wreckers." *Detroit Free Press*. 10 December 1949.

22. "Chautauqua Plans Assuming Form." *Northville Record*. 29 June 1917.

23. "1917 Chautauqua Gratifying Success." *Northville Record*. 3 August 1917.

24. *Northville Record*. January 1877.

25. *Northville Record*. 10 February 1877.

26. *Northville Record*. 13 July 1878.

27. "Northville Is Going to Have Talkies." *Northville Record*. 13 September 1929.

28. Barfknecht, Gary. *Michellaneous II*. pp. 173–174.

CHAPTER TEN

1. *Detroit Free Press*. 12 June 1849.

2. "Changed Hands." *Wayne County Record*. 13 November 1869.

3. Utley, Henry. *Michigan Pioneer & Historical Collections* (1882): Vol. 5, pp. 242–248.

4. Clarkson, David. "Pioneer Sketches." Burton Historical Collection, Detroit Public Library.

5. *Northville Record*. 6 December 1907.

6. "Fire Destroys Oldest Landmark of Village." *Northville Record*. 13 December 1929.

7. Hoffman, Jack. *Northville: The First Hundred Years*. p. 120.

8. *Northville Record*. 10 June 1871.

9. *Detroit Free Press*. 9 October 1865.

10. Schramm, Jack E., William H. Heming, and Richard R. Andrews. *When Eastern Michigan Rode the Rails, Book III*. p. 37.

11. Ibid., p. 82.

12. "Auto Show Big Feature of the Fair." *Northville Record*. 13 September 1929.

13. "Eddie Stinson Flies from Here to Syracuse, 2 hrs 32 minutes." *Northville Record*. 24 February 1928.

14. Unidentified, undated Toledo, Ohio newspaper clipping.

EPILOGUE

1. Serling, Rod. "A Stop at Willoughby." *More Stories from the Twilight Zone*. p. 111.

The old bandstand, or "crow's nest," standing at the corner of Center and Main Streets evokes an image and feeling of Northville's romantic past.

INDEX